1720

EAST WOODROW STREET

The Alvin W. Johnson Story

1720

EAST WOODROW STREET

The Alvin W. Johnson Story

BY ALVIN W. JOHNSON

Lethal Weapon
PRISON MINISTRIES

1720 East Woodrow Street
The Alvin W. Johnson Story

ISBN-13: 978-0-9847821-9-2

Printed in the United States of America
March 2016

APPTE Publishing, Atlanta, Georgia

PRISON MINISTRIES
P.O. Box 920651
Norcross, Georgia 30010
www.Lethalweaponministries.org

The following versions of the Bible are used in this book:

Cover design by Marshall Grant

DEDICATION

This book is dedicated to the GIVER of GRACE and
the MINISTER of RECONCILIATION. I thank the
Lord Jesus Christ for his saving grace and love for me.
This book is also dedicated to my wife Marya,
My brothers David J. Johnson,
Marvel Johnson, and Joe L. Johnson
In loving memory of my parents,
the Rev. Holloway Johnson and Maxine L. Johnson
and my two sons,
Alvin S. Johnson and Alonzo C. J. Johnson
And especially to all my relatives and friends

ACKNOWLEDGMENTS

I would like to thank my spiritual dad Bishop Wellington Boone for inspiring me to write this book. Bishop Boone gave me a word on my first day at his church, The Father's House in Norcross, Georgia, that really spoke to my heart. It caught my attention because it gave me what I really needed at that time—a ministerial covering and a spiritual dad.

God had just delivered me from a 25-year crack addiction and an additional 10 years with other drugs. I had found a church that speaks the truth without compromising and the truth penetrated my heart that day. The Word of God was rooted in my heart and I was set free.

Thank you, Bishop, for believing in me and not giving up on me as others had done in the past. I have not had anyone believe in me or speak into my life like Bishop Boone. It was a word that would last for eternity, if I received it the right way.

I remember that day after church when just he and I were talking. I was sitting directly in front of him and he was telling me things that no one had ever said to me about how God was going to use me. Fear came over me along with excitement and I didn't know how to explain that. I never in my life had heard anybody who was so encouraging. It was nothing but the Holy Spirit working through him.

I kept saying in the back of my mind, *Who is this man? I have never seen God use anybody at this level.* That's because I had been so far away from God and his presence that I had forgotten what it looked like. I love this man so much that I am willing to lay down my life for him.

It has been more than 10 years since I started serving under a man of God who can be used to reach and change the whole world. At the right time he licensed me as a minister in the Fellowship of International Churches, an organization he founded. I have so much respect for Bishop Boone because he doesn't *make* you do anything he asks but he wants you to do it willingly because it's what God wants out of your life.

I also want to thank Bishop's editor Cynthia Ellenwood for pushing me for the past years to complete this book without giving up. She was so encouraging and aggressive and really stayed on me over and over again until I got it right. She really pushes me and it paid off. I also want to thank three other editors for their invaluable contributions, Catrina Frison, Malaka Grant and Patrice Jones.

The prayers of my father also prevailed for my life even after he had gone home to be with the Lord, which manifested in my rededicating my life back to Jesus.

I want to thank Pastor Lawrence "Doc" Reed whom I first met in a Wendy's fast-food restaurant. He took a real interest in me from that day on. I had just given my life to the Lord after 18 years of running. He told me about the Father's House in Norcross, Georgia, and Bishop Wellington Boone.

When I met Bishop Boone I was surprised that God had led me to a man of God who reminded me of my biological dad, but sometimes it's so much harder, because of familiarity, to listen to your family members who are saved. That's not the case all the time, but sometimes you barely listen to them. If it wasn't for the teachings and the time Bishop Boone has spent with me, I probably wouldn't be here today because of my rebellion against God and my disobedience.

I love you, Bishop, for being the real deal and being a light to all Christians. You represent the kingdom of God in a mighty way by living by God's principles and Jesus' standards.

ALVIN W. JOHNSON

CONTENTS

FOREWORD BY BISHOP WELLINGTON BOONE

Alvin Johnson is a prison evangelist and also a spiritual father. Men receive Christ and stay saved after they are released because he continues to call them, confront them, and teach them how to live righteously, as God has taught him. He is the kind of Christian man we are all called to be."

If you ever heard Alvin tell the stories that you will read about in this book, you would think they were impossible, but his wife Marya and his oldest brother David back him up completely. They all lived through it—the trials as well as the triumphs. It's a true story of the amazing power of God.

The first time Alvin walked in the church doors more than a decade ago, he was in such bad physical shape from past drugs and debauchery that he had to struggle just to walk on crutches. Within a short time, because he had given his life to Jesus, God healed him and he threw away the crutches.

Over the next few years, he went through one life-threatening health crisis after another but he fought back with faith, and The Father's House Church in Norcross, Georgia, fought with him.

During that time, Alvin went back to prison—no longer an inmate but now winning people to Jesus by the hundreds. He did the same thing on the streets. To this day he has probably brought more visitors to our church than everyone else put together. In all those years, he never once backslid.

I have watched Alvin become so transformed by his encounter with Jesus Christ that I believe what he says that someday he will be reaching the world.

His greatest victories happen in the prisons. Last year alone, with no staff but other volunteers like him and little financial backing, through the ministry he started called Lethal Weapon Prison Ministries, he personally led hundreds of men and women to Christ. He also got a job working with juveniles and gave them love and godly standards and they were changed.

Bishop Garland Hunt, the former president of Prison Fellowship whom I installed in my place last year as senior pastor of The Father's House, knows what it takes to reach men in prison. He told me that Alvin is bringing a revolution. Not only that, but Alvin remains under submission to Bishop Hunt as his pastor and comes to church every Sunday morning before he and the team go to the prisons later that day.

When Pastor Lawrence "Doc" Reed first met Alvin in a fast-food restaurant and invited him to our church, Alvin needed some correction as he made the transformation from sinner to saint. He respected me as a father and he had the grace to listen and do what I said. Something good was still inside of him from his past discipleship by his dad and the power of the Holy Spirit.

When we disciple someone as a father, we are always his father and he is always our son. The Apostle Paul said in 1 Corinthians 4:15, "For though ye have ten thousand instructors in Christ, yet have ye not many fathers: for in Christ Jesus I have begotten you through the gospel."

In this book, read carefully how Alvin's father never abandoned his wife and family and you will understand what happens when a father raises his sons according to biblical principles. Eventually Alvin and his brothers returned to the Lord and now all are ministers because of a godly father.

Alvin is a great example of what I call "Street Revs." Once he leaves the church, everyone he meets is going to hear about Jesus. A Street Rev is not only an evangelist but also an example of Christ-likeness. He gets people saved, then lives a godly life before them.

Each of us needs to be willing to look honestly at our own sin. We need to look with an unwavering gaze on the way that God judges unrighteousness. The world wants to make excuses for our sin so that they can excuse their own, but God gives us love plus standards that change men's lives forever. That is his message and that is his lifestyle.

In closing, I want to say that Alvin and his father are examples to me of what can happen in Black America once Black men are converted and live for Christ. When I see Black men like them, I am encouraged that my race is about to wake up from our spiritual slumber and see that the devil and some of our own Black leaders have been tricking us into becoming our own worst enemy by shifting our focus away from God.

The predominantly Black prison population shows what happens when men are fatherless and lack vision for their own God-given value. They become a burden on America by crime, sexual sin, and abandoning their families. However, I believe that Alvin Johnson is one man who can reverse this curse.

To Alvin—God bless you, son!

It is my prayer that God will use this book as a vehicle to multiply your impact on those in prison and also to challenge men in the churches to go out now and reach the lost for Jesus, then father them into Christ-likeness. May this be the beginning of a worldwide impact that empties prisons and transforms churches and communities. In Jesus' name I pray. Amen!

BISHOP WELLINGTON BOONE
Chief Prelate, Fellowship of International Churches

INTRODUCTION BY ALVIN W. JOHNSON.
IT'S FINALLY OVER!

I took all the money that my wife Marya and I needed to pay the rent—$600—and walked to the Village Inn Motel near our apartment in Norcross, Georgia, to get high. For the next four days I was getting high in that motel room and spending money like it would be my last day on earth. I bought crack cocaine and we drank a half gallon of vodka. I was strung out on a binge and craving for crack cocaine like never before. I was filthy dirty and nasty and my hair was nappy. I didn't change underwear at all in four days, or even think about brushing my teeth or taking a bath.

As soon as the drug dealer at the motel got all my money he started pushing me to leave. When I wouldn't go, we got into an argument about my begging so much. He snarled, "Go home, nigger, or else we're going to kill you. You have a good woman at home, so leave!"

I tried to bargain with him. I pleaded, "Give me another hit and then I'll leave." I got myself a big hit but I couldn't feel anything and there was no high. I drank more vodka but I still couldn't feel a thing. I would think I was high and then I would think I wasn't.

"Give me my money back," I yelled. "Or give me some more crack cocaine." I was ready to die for another hit. I wanted that other hit so bad that I didn't care about anyone— my wife, my friends, or even God.

For a moment something came over me and I thought I heard a voice . . . but I didn't think it was God because I hadn't heard God's voice in more than 18 years! If he had spoken to me during those years, I was in so much sin that I probably couldn't have recognized his voice, anyway.

Suddenly, out of nowhere, I heard an inner voice.

The voice said, *"It's over."*

Immediately I got up and started walking home. Everybody thought I had whacked out from that hit, and so did I. I walked down Pinnacle Way to Beaver Ruin and then I heard this voice say again. *"It's over."*

What? I thought in my head this must be some good dope or I am really high and tripping. But now I'm trying to figure out if it was actually the real voice of the Lord speaking to me. I didn't recognize his voice anymore but for some reason I broke out crying. *It was really over."*

By the time I made it home, guilt was all over me. I was broken and Marya was so mad at me for taking the rent money that she had made up her mind to move away from me for good. Our friends Cliff and Mary Price were helping her pack up her things. I begged her to forgive me and all I could say was *"It's over. I promise it's over."* Those words just kept coming out of my mouth.

It would be a miracle if Marya believed me after all that I had put her through since we had been together. She had made a list of all my failures in our relationship. With all honesty I have to admit that was me! I was a typical drug addict. This is what she listed that I had been doing:

Smoke dope

Always conning me

Lie too much about money

Irresponsible

Selfish

Never do what you say when you say it

We never do activities together—except sleeping in bed

Love hanging out with your THUG friends instead of POSITIVE people

Never set goals

Disrespectful—Hang out till the next day—morning

Undermine me

Maybe she will calm down if I go outside, I thought. I went outside, but while I was out there the power of God moved in again and this time *he took control.*

As I was sitting on the steps leading from my apartment, I looked up and saw a form of something standing by a bush and this form was motioning for me to come over to where it was. I was so afraid I couldn't even look at it. I thought about Moses and the burning bush.

As I kept sitting there, it seemed like the Holy Spirit grabbed me and picked me up and moved me over by that bush. I knelt down. I didn't know if it was an out-of-body experience or what.

Then I heard the voice of Jesus say, *"I will never leave you or forsake you."* Then I felt a touch on my head and I felt an anointing like never before in my life. In an instant the power of God had changed my whole heart. It was a supernatural experience!

Wow! I got up and started running back into the apartment yelling, *"It's over! It's over! It's over!"* Nothing else would come out of my mouth. Marya shouted, "Call the police! This fool has gone crazy!"

But they never called the police. I was still scared after that supernatural intervention but I knew without a shadow of a doubt that it was nothing but Jesus intervening in my life.

I got on the phone with my brother and asked if he could send me the rent money that I had just wasted. My brother's response astonished me. He said, "What you need to do is get on your knees and tell God you are sorry for turning your back on him. Repent and ask for forgiveness."

"It's over," I told him. "It's finally over." (It would be a while before I told him my testimony about the details of that divine intervention and what really happened to me.)

"I'll think about sending you the rent money," my brother said. I know he didn't want to send any money because Marya had been telling him that every time he sent me money I would smoke it up in dope. Dope addicts are always convincing the person who is sending the money that they are serious about their need and how they will change this time. They are so determined and so desperate to fulfill their want that they will make up any story or tell a serious lie that is believable.

An addict has to just get out of denial and admit that you have a problem and that you need help. Eventually it is God who delivers you but he has given man the ability to create systems and put them in place for us such as Alcohol Anonymous, Narcotics Anonymous, rehabs, support groups, and most of all family support, which is so vitally important.

Miraculously, I talked Marya into staying. After she had calmed down and gone to the bedroom, I got on my knees and was awake all night praying as I had never prayed before in my life. I was that serious in my heart about really changing.

The power of God had just manifested in my life and this time I asked God to take everything out of my heart that was not of him and remove it permanently—all the worldly things. I told him that I would surrender my life to him only, in the name of Jesus. From twelve o'clock that night until six o'clock the next morning, I was on my knees weeping and crying out to God until I finally fell asleep.

When I woke up it was already about noon. I got up and flushed down the toilet all the dope and every bit of weed I had left. I even threw away my cigarettes and poured out all the liquor. I also got rid of all the secular music with its ungodly messages promoting sin.

After 35 years of being strung out on drugs, I finally gave it all to God and I have never looked back. I have lived the last 11 years totally sold out for Jesus and for most of those years I have been writing this book.

This book is not for me. It's for you, the reader.

If God did this for me, and it has lasted like this, I know He will do it for you. If you don't have the answers for your life, there is a God you can turn to who created your life and knows everything about you. The truth is, as he said, that he knew you before you were in your mother's womb.

Give Jesus your life. You just have to trust him and not try him and your whole life will be changed. I'll take that to the bank, as they say.

Personally, I had been court-ordered to A.A. (Alcohol Anonymous), N.A. (Narcotics Anonymous), rehab centers—you name it—but they did not work for me. I really hadn't tried Jesus in a real way. I don't knock programs that are working for other people. I'm just sharing my testimony about how Jesus beat out all the others.

See, for me, surrendering to Jesus and putting him first was something that l hadn't done and that's where I personally went wrong. I should have known better with my background in a godly family and the church, but I didn't.

Now I have to give him all the honor and glory for giving me so many chances to get it right. Tell me which is better—surrendering to Almighty God, or to the police?

I thank everyone who has been a part of my life through my struggles. I am telling you that there are people who can be witnesses that what I am about to tell you is true. They will tell you that I never looked back or fell back.

I can sum up my life story in one Scripture, Romans 8:28, *"And we know that all things work together for good to them that love God, to them who are the called according to his purpose" (KJV).*

This book is a testimony of my love for God and God's undying love and unmerited favor to someone who *least* deserved it—me. It tells how a heavenly Father stepped into a sinner's life and transformed him, changed a man's heart, and brought salvation.

However, more than just my story, it is the story of my family and how God brought us through childhood years with a mentally ill mother. The police never wanted to take that call to the Johnson home. You will see why they reacted that way after reading this book. But God! What a great example we had in my dedicated father whom I always saw on his knees before day and again late at night. This is a story of a real father who loved God and loved and wife and sons.

This is one family's story of redemption.

It is my story. I'm Alvin, the youngest of the family, and I'm here to share the story of the Johnson family.

CHAPTER 1.

BAD PREACHER'S KIDS

Holloway and Maxine Johnson

It was in the early 1950s when my father, Holloway Johnson, met and married my mother, Maxine Louise Williams. At the time they were married, my father was a drinker, a gambler, and a former Golden Glove boxer.

He was 5 foot 8 inches tall and stocky with wavy black hair, weighed about 220 pounds, had blue eyes with radiant skin, and was strong as an ox. My dad did not play. He meant what he said.

My mom was about 5 feet 7 inches tall and had beautiful long black hair and a radiant skin complexion. She was so beautiful back in the day and maintained her beauty throughout the years of the mental illness I will tell you about in this book.

My mom told us to trust in the Lord and never give up. Mom and Dad made a beautiful couple. My mom was sweet as gold when she wasn't sick, but when she was off her medicine you better have a hiding place or safe escape route.

After they were married they purchased a home in the famous Greenwood Black business district of Tulsa, Oklahoma, on 536 East King just off Greenwood Avenue and had four sons together—David, Marvel, Joel, and Alvin. We were born from 1953 through 1957.

Like all families, we had our share of happiness and heartache, joy and suffering. However, in my family there was trouble on the horizon.

With perseverance and God's grace, mercy, and protection, we were able to make it through the pain and abuse that comes from living with a mother suffering from mental illness. I call it a demonic possession, but the devil does not get any glory for what my mom put us through. God gets the glory for defeating him in our family.

Despite all the turmoil that was taking place in our home, we thought we were a normal family growing up in Oklahoma. Thirty years earlier, in the spring of 1921, race riots had hit our community and Greenwood Avenue had been burned to the ground. It was one of the worst race riots this country has ever seen. The thriving 35-block neighborhood, also known as "Black Wall Street," was looted, set ablaze, and bombed by whites who flew planes in the air and dropped 50 gallon drums of gasoline. It was the only American city that had been bombed like that.

We heard stories about John Dillinger and Pretty Boy Floyd, who were bank robbers, and how they used to hang out on Greenwood and hide bank robbery money in the walls of the Small's Hotel on Greenwood. When the whites tore it down, the elderly people in the neighborhood said that they found all kinds of money in the walls. There were rumors that money was flying in the air and lying in the streets of Greenwood.

The white vigilantes of Tulsa were bent on destroying the prosperous community of Black American businesses that had grown up in the Greenwood District.

Hundreds of black people lost their lives in that riot, driven by a little white lie, a false accusation of rape against a black man—a crime that never happened. The damage was so brutal that it seemed insurmountable, but by the 1950s when we lived there, Greenwood would be restored to reclaim some of her former glory and flourish again.

Up the street from our house, we had this big old hill where we used to play. At the top of this hill were some apartments called Greenwood Village. There was a gang in those apartments that shared the same name (Greenwood Villagers Gang) and a brickyard on the hill.

There was also a Coca-Cola Bottling Company and my brothers had to cut through to get to Charles S. Johnson Elementary School. I hadn't started school at the time.

Sturdy workmen at the brickyard would come and load up their trucks with stacks of bricks. Sometimes my mom would have us search for clay rocks on the hill because she liked to eat them. I tried one out of curiosity and it was awful. I wondered how she could crave those things.

I would wonder about a lot more of the strange things that my mom did in the years to come.

Greenwood was the spot back in the day. My brothers and I used to catch blue ring snakes and play with them on the hill. Over time, it became a contest to see who could catch the most snakes.

King's Park was just down the street where there was archery, volleyball, softball, and football, but we spent most of our time in the King's Park pool. When the older guys got in the water, we hopped right out, because they would dunk us hard and almost try to drown us, just for fun.

We also played on the railroad tracks that were near the park and we used to wait for freight trains to roll by so we could jump on them and ride for a while and then jump off. I realize now that was pretty dangerous, but you don't think about that as a kid, do you?

We had a lot of family members living nearby. My grandmother had a house next to the alleyway that led to the park. My little cousin Guan, who was four years old at the time, lived with my grandmother and he used to go with us to the park. My grandmother was his great-grandmother.

We played football with guys who were much older than we were but we played with heart and the older guys respected us for that. We loved playing in that park but we had other things going on at home that were not play.

My mom Maxine had one brother, Alvin, whom I'm named after, who lived in San Francisco. He was the youngest child in her family and the only boy.

The sisters in her family were Lula Mae, the youngest girl (San Francisco), then my mother Maxine (Tulsa), Jackie (San Francisco), and the oldest sister, Thelma (Tulsa), who ran a juke joint on Greenwood where we used to hang out as kids. We went to the juke joint when we were little and those old men and women used to give us quarters and fifty-cent pieces to cut a rug (dance).

Our cousin Wimpy was a gangster back in those days, 6 foot 4 inches tall, 250 pounds, and solid as a rock. My brothers and my cousin Guan and I used to watch him fight on Greenwood.

When older guys who hung around the neighborhood used to mess with us, we would say that we were going to get Wimpy to protect us. He was in his 20s and we called him "Uncle" because he was much older than we were. He really was our cousin and Guan's uncle but when those guys found out Wimpy was some kin to us they would beg us not to tell him because he had a reputation for doing damage.

Wimpy's sister Valerie had a bad reputation, too. She didn't take any mess. We knew her by the name Aunt Sally and we were terrified of her when we were little kids.

I have to admit that we were bad kids when we were little. After my dad became a man of God we were bad Preacher's Kids.

My dad started preaching in 1965 when he became a man on fire for God after he almost died and made a deal with the Lord. I was about five years old at the time he was saved and for the rest of the years we were growing up he made us four boys read the Bible every day and quote Scriptures, and explain what God was saying, and what that meant to us.

Dad didn't know all of the bad things we were doing but he knew enough to pray for us on his knees. He lived by Scriptures like Psalm 118:8 (KJV) that says, *"It's better to trust in the Lord than to put your confidence in man."*

Other kids in the neighborhood were bad, too, and we had to fight most of the time. If someone attacked us and we didn't fight back and ran home, my mom would make us go right back outside to fight them.

We used to climb on the top of our neighbor's roof and jump from that house to our house all the time. On one occasion we all decided to jump one by one across the rooftops so we all climbed up on top of the house.

David went first and made it. Marvell jumped next and was successful. Joe jumped next. He was wearing some cardboard wings that David had made for him as if he were going to fly but Joe went hurtling down the side of those houses and hit the gas meter.

After I saw that, there was no way I was going to jump. I turned around and went back. I knew for sure my legs weren't nearly as long or strong as his were. Joe was blessed that afternoon because he survived with only cuts and bruises. We never tried that again and I think we never told my dad about that incident.

In 1963 when I was five years old, we finally moved to our new home at 1720 East Woodrow Street in North Tulsa, the title of this book and the place where all the chaos began. It's a place I'll never forget as long as I live. My parents lived there for 42 years.

At that time, my dad was working a lot at Southwestern Bell Telephone Company and Red Top, a janitorial company at Hillcrest Medical Center, and my mom was a devoted housewife, the best she knew how.

When we were young, my dad would always tell us about our mother's symptoms and instruct us to pay close attention to any behavior that seemed out of the ordinary and check in with him periodically at work.

Woods Elementary was being built next door to our house in 1965 and we used to play on the construction site among the nearby stacks of metal, pipes, and all of the debris.

One day David, Marvel, and Joe got on one end of a big pipe and told me to go down to the other end of the pipe and start yelling, so like a fool I started yelling into the pipe.

In the meantime, while I was yelling, they rolled a large rock through the opening of their end of the pipe. The echo from my yelling muffled the sound of the rock traveling so I couldn't hear the rock coming at me. All of a sudden the rock hit me dead in my mouth and nose. Blood sprayed everywhere and I started hollering.

Whenever they did anything bad to me they would always tell me not to tell. I was always the easiest target by being the youngest. They would promise me candy or anything I wanted. So when I got home I told my dad I fell on my face while I was running.

We used to stay in the house a lot until we got to know the other kids on the block, and we would also try to shield my mother's mental condition from the new neighbors.

My mom managed to get loose a couple of times, and that's when my dad started introducing himself to the neighbors, telling them about our mother's condition.

We started going to Ralph J. Bunch Elementary where my Aunt Mert taught school until Woods Elementary was finished in 1965. I knew I would like Woods because the back door was right at the side door of our home. However, it turned out to be not so convenient when I got a real taste of my mom's "symptoms" during a school day at Woods.

My dad had always tried to help manage my mom's sickness but in spite of all of his efforts I eventually became the laughingstock of my first grade class.

When I was about seven years old, I was sitting in class when suddenly there was a big crash and my mother busted into class, tearing the door off the wall like Superman and throwing it on the ground! Then she stood there in front of all my friends. She was buck naked!

My teacher and my classmates were so shocked you could hear a pin drop. I was shocked speechless and totally embarrassed. All I wanted to do was slither under my desk and disappear.

The teacher called the principal on the intercom to come immediately to the room and when he came they told me to take her home. I did not return that day!

After my classmates got over the shock they burst out laughing and teased me mercilessly from then on. Kids can be really cruel when they don't understand something, and they didn't understand my mother's condition. How could they? I figured if I could get past that, I could get past anything. It's a wonder I still have my sanity!

My oldest brother David could be really cruel at times. We also fought among ourselves. My dad had set David in charge of all of us boys and commanded David to keep us out of trouble. However, David did just the opposite.

My dad was at work one day when David had done something to all of us. I can't remember what it was. We decided to get together and jump him, but he was too much for us. He charged all of us at once, knocked us into a clothes closet, and somehow locked us in.

It was noon when he locked us in that closet and we were there until my dad got ready to come home from work late that evening.

My mom was in the hospital at that time. A lot of mischief went on when my mom was in the hospital and we boys were home alone. When my mom had breakdowns she would be in the hospital for one or two months at a time, or longer. We would drive to see her all the way to Taft Mental Institution, in Taft, Oklahoma.

Sometimes I was scared to travel there because some of those patients would mess with us and try to get in our car when we were leaving the hospital. We would lock our doors and my dad would tell them they needed to please go back in and stay there.

Apart from being scared, I enjoyed the ride. It took about one and a half hours to get there, but you know that's long when you are kids. When it was time to go home, I hated to leave my mom in that place and as little kids do, we always cried when we left her.

When my mom came home from the hospital, we didn't know how to act. We were so happy! Even when it was time to go to bed and my parents were asleep, we would wake them with some foolishness just to see her.

Sometimes it didn't work out so well to wake them up. David used to sit back on the bed, bend his knees, and tell us to sit on his feet while he held our arms to balance us. Then he would push his legs straight out and shoot us up in the air like a rocket and we would hit the other bed across the room. We would all take turns and as usual it was always some mess when it came to me.

I sat on David's legs and he pushed me harder than Marvel and Joe. I flew all the way to the top of the ceiling, hit it, and then hit the wall and slid down, waking my mom and dad. We came very close to getting a whipping, but after we explained what happened, they went to bed laughing, and I went to bed bruised.

We always had something going on at night. One time Joe made all of us get a whipping.

We young boys would get up at night to use the rest room and I guess Joe would hear us leaving the other bedroom. He would sneak out in the hallway that went to the bathroom and get on all fours like an animal. On our way to the bathroom he would make a wild sound in the dark like a cat screaming or something. We would jump and yell out loud and since it was the middle of the night it would wake up my mom and dad, and that was it!

My dad would cut on that light with his hand on the belt and we would plead with him, "Dad, it wasn't me, that was Joe!" But sometimes we would all get it.

We always did things to each other, like putting shoes or cups of water on the top of the door while it was cracked open, and then one of us would call the other one to come in the room. The rest of us would sit there and wait while they came and opened the door and whatever would be at the top of the door would fall on the top of his head.

We would start laughing, but even with that, we didn't always get away with our actions. Sometimes we would explain what had happened, and my mom and dad couldn't help but laugh. Sometimes that would save us.

The Ten Commandments says, *"Honor your father and mother. Then you will live a long, full life in the land the Lord your God is giving you"* (Exodus 20:12 NLT).

I learned the hard way. You have to obey them, and it doesn't matter how old you get, you still need to have the utmost respect for them.

Mom and Dad never heard my brothers or me say one curse word to them or argue with them in their entire lives, and that's the truth. As bad as I was, I still respected them.

Whenever my mom was sick and my dad was going through it, after he was saved he was crying out before the Lord, yelling and calling on the name of Jesus. I used to hear him say all the time, "Lord, help us through!" and not one time did he ever give up from the pressure. He always remained humble and had patience with my mom.

It was amazing for me to see that while I was growing up. I should have turned out better than I did with such a Christ-like example. For me to have lived a worldly and carnal-minded life the way I used to in those days, with a dad like that, is a disgrace before God. We were bad Preacher's Kids, as I said, and we were getting even worse.

Eventually Marvel had Joe and me skipping school and he used to have us go up to the TG&Y Department Store to steal toys. Marvel became a good thief at that time but I almost got caught after the manager realized we were playing hooky and stealing.

One time when we were on our way to steal, there was a big field across from us and Marvel had us playing with matches. We would light the grass on fire and when the fire started to get big we would put it out with our feet. We kept doing that until one day the circle got too big to put out and we took off running all the way home.

When we looked at that field the next day, the whole field was burned up—about five acres of land. We never did tell anybody that we did it.

I actually learned to have an aversion to stealing. My brother Joe stole a collar for a little dog we had called Pinto and he got caught stealing it at Walgreens.

When they called my dad at work, I knew that stealing was over for me, especially after my dad got home and beat Joe half to death. I despise stealing to this day.

The school called about us playing hooky and when the truant officer came to our house she scared me so bad I think I pissed on myself. She came in that house and threatened to take me! I held onto my brother David's leg and wouldn't let go, screaming, "Don't let her take me!"

Marvel really made us get our butts beat with that one, and every bit of this took place while my mom was in the mental ward.

We were bad preacher's kids, but that is just the beginning of this story.

CHAPTER 2.

ALERT ON EAST WOODROW STREET

When people moved into our neighborhood who didn't know my mom, they would lock their doors and close their curtains and wouldn't come outside at all when she was sick. Eventually most of them started coming around my mom more often and it was apparent that they had adjusted to her being sick. We got to know them and after we were a part of the neighborhood they began to understand my mom. Everyone on the street helped, and we became close to them.

We had the Dangerfields, the Knuals, the Morrows, the Johnsons, the Williams, the Allens, the Scotts, the Murphys, the Mayberrys, and the Gaines, who are relatives on my mom's side of the family. I hung with my cousin Sunny Gaines a lot. He had a motorcycle and I would ride on the back of it wherever he went. We used to be all over Tulsa and the surrounding towns. Unfortunately, Sunny had me fooling with older women, too, but that's another story.

I had a friend Rickey in my class who lived around the corner. His mother, Mrs. Earline Edwards, had been one of my mom's classmates. My mom would go there to relax because Mrs. Edwards could always calm her down.

I gained several other friends from the neighborhood. Barney Mason and his cousin Wendell were my best friends in school. My mom fixed bologna sandwiches for us every day. Wendell and I still have great communication with each other. We have been friends for 50 years.

Barney and I were raised like brothers. Barney's mom took me in every time my mom went to the hospital and raised me like one of her own sons. I am so grateful for that. Also, Momma Charlene Perkins watched over me many times along with her two sons Fontain and Kenny.

My Aunt Mert lived up the street. When my mom got sick and tore up our house, she went to my Aunt Mert's house and left the mess for us to clean up. Mom also went to the Dangerfields who lived directly across the street from us and to my relatives in the Gaines family.

When Mom got there she would yell out their names in a booming voice and say things like, "Hurry up and open the door, God d_____!" She would scare everybody.

While she was sick she would be talking "noise," telling us kids that she would cut our mother f____ throats. She would be serious. Other kids would say that she was just playing and we would say, "No! She's not playing!" They would ask if our mom would do that to her own kids, and we would say to them that they just didn't understand. Then we would have to explain what she was like.

The Dangerfields became our closest helpers on the street and we considered them cousins after a while. Mrs. Dangerfield was good to us. She was like a second mom and she worked in the public school system. When my mom was in the hospital, she would make sure we had a free lunch at school so sometimes we would hold on to our lunch money that my dad had left for us until after school and go to the candy store.

Sometimes we had to stay all night with the Dangerfields because dad was doing janitorial work at his night job. After work Dad would pick us up from the Dangerfields. He used to bring us Cracker Jacks all the time after work and we were always excited to see what kind of prize was in the box. He also brought us jelly donuts. Dad would put cheese on his. I still love jelly donuts.

Mrs. Dangerfield's husband was like a dad to us, too, and he would whip us like we were his own. We called him Big Bird. They were a nice looking family, close-knit, with three girls and two boys. They really had their family together.

The girls were "fine" and they are still beautiful to this day. My brother Marvel used to give them peanut butter and jelly sandwiches in exchange for kisses and when we saw him get that first kiss, we all were making sandwiches.

My dad started saying, "Boy, you all sure are going through a lot of bread. I just bought bread last night!" We told him what Marvel was doing but we didn't tell him that we were a part of it, too.

The other neighbors embraced us, but not like the Dangerfields. They were special to us and still are today, because they were truly a blessing. I will always love them and they will always have a special place in my heart. I try my best to visit the Dangerfields' house every time I go home to Tulsa. I will never forget them, as long as I live.

We stayed up the hill on a dead end street along with the Knuals, Dangerfields, Buchanans, and Mosleys. The Mosleys' three girls could never play with us because their parents were strict and they could only play in their yard.

We used to call ourselves the Hillbillies. We called the people downhill the Twilight Zone. When we got in arguments, we would forget that we had to walk down the street past them to get to the store. The Twilight people would scare us and say, "Back up that hill, you Hillbillies!"

Sometimes my brother David and the Dangerfield boys had to walk with us, because the Twilight People would try to jump us. We always took up for each other. They didn't mess with us too much because they knew Momma Mac (the name the Dangerfields gave to my mom) might remember what they did to us when she got sick and go down and terrorize the Twilight Zone. Everybody knew my mom was not a joke. She was dangerous.

We all ended up staying at each other's houses a lot, helping each other out and playing together all the time. One time we built a tin shack playhouse we called the Sugar Shack. We made homemade furniture and brought in some old used furniture, and it was nice. All of the kids up on the hill used to meet there but it was off limits to the Twilight people because it was our personal clubhouse.

One night the Twilight people tore down our playhouse and we had to rebuild it. The final day we played there was when we ran in there to get out of the rain and it started to thunder. A huge lightning bolt hit that shack. We all ran home, and that was the end of the Sugar Shack. We never went in there again, and eventually we tore it down.

My mother's and dad's families were very supportive of my mom and were always concerned about her. I will never forget my family because they shared the pain with us. They are very special to me.

The women in the family were not afraid to do battle with my mom when she got sick. They were rough women. They didn't take any mess. My mom's family and my dad's family could back up every bit of it. My mom's family had plenty of weapons such as shotguns and hand guns, knives— you name it, they had it. They used to carry weapons in their back pocket. They loved the Lord but if you messed with them the wrong way, they would help you *see* the Lord.

At times my dad used to take us over to Ponca City, Oklahoma, so he could see his brothers. He was raised there as a child after his family left Taylor, Mississippi. On the way over to Ponca we used to stop in Fairfax, Oklahoma, to see one of his brothers named L.T. We would visit with him awhile and then move on to Ponca, which was about an hour's drive from Tulsa. We always had to go to church in Ponca just like we did in Tulsa, because four of my dad's brothers were also preachers at that time. A couple of my dad's brothers moved to Los Angeles, California. Another one stayed in Denver and the oldest stayed in Tulsa where we lived.

My mom told us about one time before my dad got saved that he got in a fight with a man on Greenwood for messing with her, and my dad hit that man so hard that he knocked all the skin off his forehead. That's when we found out that my dad was a former Golden Gloves prizefighter like his oldest brother, James "Kid Dynamite" Johnson, who was really good to us.

Sometimes we would stay at his house for a week or two, and my Aunt Katherine Johnson could fry that chicken and bake those cakes and pies, and we would eat good after coming from the park swimming and playing football. My cousin James, Jr., was a lifeguard at the pool. He was later drafted into the Marine Corps during the Vietnam War. He lost his life in the war but he had lived for the Lord even before he was drafted and served his country.

The rest of the kids were Nadine, Faye, Rita, Timothy, Floyd, Priscilla and Louis Lee, and they were comical, just like our family. I guess that was the Johnson/Martin blood line.

When the family came to Tulsa, they got to know a lot of our friends, and when we were in Ponca, we got to know a lot of their friends. They were all athletes and had track, football, and basketball trophies everywhere at home. They broke track records that still haven't been broken today.

We would sit outdoors at night and Dad and my uncle would tell us scary stories about the headless man and the half-man, half-goat. We would be too scared to go to sleep at night.

While we were there we used to go see my dad's dad, Louis "Lish" Johnson, who stayed two blocks over. I didn't mind going to see him but when we would sit in that house his wife, Momma Johnson (my step-grandmother), would have it so hot in there that we would beg dad to let us go outside. We would get nauseated from the heat, it was so hot.

Dad would say, "No! I won't be that long," but we would be there all day. My dad was a man of discipline and so loving with the biggest heart for people. I really appreciate that now, because it really paid off.

One time, we were at church with them and Momma Johnson played the piano, or at least she thought she could. Bless her heart, it was joyful noise. Boy, did we laugh, and we all got in trouble.

We always had to sing for the church. They would say, "Let's have a selection from the Johnson family."

My momma's mother, Mini "Duke" Sims, stayed on Greenwood Avenue in Tulsa and she used to keep us after school. I can barely remember her. She passed when I was little, about five or six, and I remember being there when she passed.

I only saw my mom's dad once or twice because he stayed in Fort Worth, Texas. His name was Ennis "Boy Child" Williams, as I remember. I was about 15 years old when I met him and he was a huge man. I mean, *huge*.

My Aunt Thelma and her daughter, Valerie Wilson, took care of us most of the summer. Her brother's name was Robert Williams. "Hey! That's Wimpy! Bully Wimp the Greenwood Pimp," they called him. I told you how he was a gangster and so was Valerie. They called her Black Sally, and we used to call them uncle and aunt, since they were older than we were. They finally mellowed out from that lifestyle later.

My Aunt Thelma used to take us into the country roads where they would make their moonshine. We would feed hogs, horses, bulls, and chickens, and they also taught us how to shoot rifles and pistols. We used to go there every summer. They had plenty of land, and they grew almost every kind of vegetable you could name. We ate good and healthy in those days. My aunt had a juke joint in Coweta, Oklahoma, which was 30 minutes away from Tulsa.

Before we got to the house, we used to get out of the car on this long dirt road. My aunt had a bull named Red, and we would climb the fence to the pasture where Red was, then see if we could make it to the house before he caught us. We made it every time because we would be moving.

One time my brother David jumped on the back of a donkey. When its owner hit that donkey on the butt, it threw him. We sure did laugh that day.

My family used to ride back and forth to Tulsa in the back of the truck from Coweta, sitting on a stack of potatoes that had moonshine under it. They thought we didn't know, and we never said anything. We knew when to keep our mouths shut, even as kids.

We all had to take a bath in the same water and use the same wash cloth. I remember the big white pot with the red ring around the top. We used this pot to piss in at night, and when we filled it up with piss we would throw it out the back door of the juke joint, and if we had to do number two, we would use a flashlight to go to the outhouse. It was a long way down the hill in the dark, so we always went in twos. Those were the good old days.

CHAPTER 3.

TENDER SIDE OF "MOMMA MAC"

We boys didn't know much about my mom's condition when we were children but my dad tried his best to teach us to respect her. He explained that she had a mental condition that would not allow her to hold a steady job.

Dad especially cautioned us not to mention anything about my brother Joe getting burned when he was a baby, before we moved from E. King St., because it would bring back memories that really upset her.

This is how that all happened with Joe.

My brother David was about five or six years old when Joe got his eye burnt. David was supposed to be watching Joe in a rocking chair in the living room while my mom was in the kitchen frying some chicken for dinner.

After a while she didn't hear them playing in the living room so she went to check on Joe to make sure he was all right. What she found was a mother's worst nightmare. David had left the room. Joe was alone and when she got to the living room little Joe was lying face down in a pile of hot coals in our fireplace, not making a sound.

Momma ran over and snatched him up with trembling hands and began to wipe the ashes from his face. He wasn't crying or fussing. She was relieved and continued to wipe ash and dust from his face with her apron until she realized that his skin was peeling off with every stroke of her apron.

Momma was horrified! She took off yelling, crying, screaming, and running down the street, clutching her baby so tightly in her arms that it left a permanent mark around his left eye from the hot coals even till this day.

Later Joe had to get a skin graft from his thigh to help replace the skin around his left eye. The scars from the skin graft are still there.

The scars to my mom's mind from that shock never left, either.

I learned more about my mom's sickness from her niece and her older sister. They said that after my parents were married my mom had five miscarriages—all boys—and the doctors told her she could not bear kids. Fortunately, one of the doctors tried a procedure on my mom so that she could have kids, though she still had excruciating pain with the birth of my oldest brother David. She had a breakdown after that birth, but everyone thought that the worst breakdown she

had—the one that affected her mind for the rest of her life—
came when she found my brother Joe in the fire.

My dad always said that his kids were a gift from God
because my mother wasn't supposed to have children. She loved
all of us and he honored the Lord for letting the last four out
of nine boys survive.

My dad had strong core family values and he trusted in
the Lord. He believed that if a man had kids that he should
raise them, also. He didn't want another man whipping his kids.

By the time we were teenagers in the 70s, we had settled
in well with the neighborhood around East Woodrow Street I
was 13, Joe, 14, Marvel 16, and my eldest brother David, 17. My
dad was "Rev" and my mom was known as "Momma Mac,"
short for Maxine.

When my brothers David and Marvel were in Booker T.
Washington High School, Marvel was in the marching band at
Booker T. and David played football and wrestled and was
good at both. Joe and I were in Marion Anderson Junior High,
which they had just left. We all went to Marion Anderson,
about a three-mile walk from our home, but in ninth grade I
got bussed to Cleveland Junior High.

When David was in the twelfth grade he landed a job at
Southwestern Bell Telephone Company where my dad worked.

It was after football season and when David got his first paycheck he started smoking weed and cigarettes.

He came in the house one weekend night after getting paid. We were all in the room and David pulled out a lid of weed. That's what they called it back in the 70s. We went to the bedroom to watch David roll up a joint of weed and we told him that Momma was going to wake up and come in.

My dad was working two jobs at the time. We knew he wasn't going to get up unless we were making a lot of noise but we knew Momma would wake up at times, and she did. Marvel had asked David to roll him a joint and David told us Momma knew he smoked. Marvel said, "She knows I smoke, too." Both of them were lying.

Guess what? My mom opened that door as David was handing Marvel a joint, and Marvel, thinking fast, said, "What are you handing that to me for? I don't mess with that stuff!"

Momma said, "Boy, is that pot?" She closed the door and went back in her room where my dad was and started to cry. Joe and I said to my brother, "I thought she knew?"

We could hear my dad asking my mom, "Honey, what's wrong?" But, my mom never told him. She was protective of us at times.

My dad still had love for my mom even when she was sick. She and my dad were so in love. They used to play dominoes almost every night. My mom didn't go too many places because she might have been embarrassed about some of the things she had done before to somebody in the street.

We met kids from other schools who had heard stories about our mom and they knew my dad was a preacher. You know how word gets around.

My dad would drop us off at different friends' places or relatives' houses, and everybody was crazy about him and respected him as a preacher. They called him Uncle Holloway and he would always witness to them about Jesus and talk to all of our friends who weren't saved or going to church.

When my mom was sick and my dad wasn't home she would contradict what he had said to us. She would say things like, "Long as he held you all up from where you needed to go, you all don't have to go to church on Sunday," and my friends would just break out laughing.

Other than the bad stuff, my mom could say some of the funniest things. When my oldest brother's daughter Latisha came home from college, she would come by and see my mom. One time when she came by, I just happened to be there. Mom was "sick" at the time and she was trying to get a ride somewhere. Latisha tried to sneak away. She was well aware of how mom was at the time.

Latisha had left her classmates in the car to be safe and she tried to make it out the door but my mom caught her. "Oh, Lord!" I heard her say, and I started laughing.

"Where are you going?" my mom demanded. "Wait a minute. Give me a ride."

"Granny, I'm with some friends."

"So what? You can't give me a ride? What the hell are they, lions, tigers, and bears?"

We fell out on the floor laughing.

When my mom got really sick, she would run out of that house buck naked, like she did when I was in elementary school and she came to my class. When she had to go to the hospital for a while, we would tell her about the things she did and she would tell us to quit lying, that we knew she didn't do that. We would say, "Momma, yes you did!"

I saw a lot of good in my mom and the way she tried to help people when she was not sick. I remember one time when my mom picked up one of her friends to take her to the hospital. As soon as she arrived at the emergency room she said she heard a big thump on the floor. When she looked in the back seat, her friend was on the floor board, dead! That really set her off. She had to go to the mental ward herself after that. All I'm saying is that just because people have mental issues doesn't mean that they can't be loving or helpful to others at times.

My brother Joe tried to grow marijuana in my mom's flower bed. She caught on to Joe because he used to water the flower bed a little too often. He was the yard man around the house. She caught Joe picking marijuana out of the flower bed one time and I heard her tell him not to grow that mess in her flower bed. After that, he stopped. Preacher's Kids!

When I was about seventeen years old, I would come home late at night and hear my mom arguing with my dad, so I would sit outside the house on the patio. She never argued when she wasn't sick, and my dad never argued period, so I would dread going in the house. I would sit on the side of that house all night smoking weed. With all of that going on, I thought I had to smoke something to cope. My dad probably understood everything but the weed. I thought that mom would eventually go to sleep but that seemed impossible when she got sick. Mom would be up for days raising hell. She would sit on the sofa with a knife, or she might have a gun. We knew better than to bother her. She would play loud music all night long. Imagine the kind of effect that had on us as kids who had to go to school the next morning. It was a living nightmare! My dad would tell us to try to sleep the best we could, but that stereo was right up against my bedroom wall.

One time I got bold. Here goes big bad Alvin. I got up so bold and went to turn down that stereo. What did I do that for? She went in that purse and before I knew it, I was turning that stereo right back up again after I saw that large knife, and I mean I turned that stereo up *quick*. As a matter of fact, I turned it up louder, and I never made that mistake again. My dad said that I should know better than to mess with that stereo when your mother is sick, and the neighbors never complained. I guess they knew not to mess with her.

We were exposed to a lot, but we were taught how to respect our elders and others. We always said, "Yes, ma'am," "No, ma'am," and "Yes, sir," "No, sir," and I still say it today, because if you didn't say that growing up, you would get beaten. I don't know what's going on with today's kids.

My dad never taught us to disrespect our mom even though when she was sick she did things to disrespect him in front of us. We learned the right example from him that carried through when we had children of our own and we had to teach them to respect her, even though it is not surprising that most of them were afraid of her.

CHAPTER 4.

EXPLAINING ABOUT MY MOM

In 1975 I graduated from high school and went in the Army. During those years, Mom was getting sick more regularly than before. While I was in basic training, I could only call home when a break was available. If you have ever been in the Army, you know how that goes.

If I called my mom when she was sick she would talk crazy about the Army: "Is anybody up there bothering you? 'Cause if they are I'm going to blow that mother f_____ place to pieces!"

I always told her I was all right, because there were a lot of times I just knew I was going to hear her come busting through those barrack doors, but she never did, thank God.

When I was away, I always worried about my mom. I was afraid that somebody would kill her out in those streets. Most of the time I didn't know what was going on back at home. Since I was in contact with my son's mom, Louise, back in the States, she would write letters to update me on everything and tell me stories about my mom.

In 1976 after Advanced Individual Training (AIT) I was assigned to Korea for my first duty station. Before I left for Korea, I wrote letters to my high school sweetheart Shardell, trying to get her back from where I messed up with her, smoking and drinking, which she didn't approve of.

Things didn't work out with Shardell, so I moved on and married my baby's momma, Louise, but that marriage only lasted for two years.

One time when I was with the Army in Korea, the Red Cross called me to say I had an emergency phone call. I just knew something tragic had happened to my mom, but instead I found out that my mom had gone out to the Red Cross and made them call me.

The nurse at the Red Cross asked me a lot of questions about my mom and I told her that I was thankful and glad she had let my mom use the phone, because she can be very dangerous. That woman said, "I wasn't being a fool. I knew she was serious, and I dialed that number in a hurry and didn't even think about getting authorization. Is she like this all the time?"

I said, "No, only when she has a nervous breakdown. She's a mental patient, and something must have upset her. I thank you for letting my mom make the call."

When I left Korea I was shipped to Fort Riley, Kansas. My dad was proud of me because he had been in the Air Force and he said every man should go into the Armed Forces for at least two years. However, after being in Fort Riley for a year, I started getting in trouble for hanging with the wrong crowd. I was arrested in 1977 and sent to Fort Leavenworth Prison in Kansas. That was my first prison term but unfortunately it would not be my last.

After I was released from Fort Leavenworth Prison I went back home. Things hadn't changed that much. Everybody was happy to see me make it back safe. We all had kids then, and we had to explain my mom's condition to them. Mom was still acting up and we were still getting calls from everybody about her—friends, neighbors, my mom's friends, my dad's friends, my friends, the police, etc. When she was on the go—we called it "the war path"—we often had to track her down.

We always tried to keep her home so that she could take her medicine. Mom hated that medicine because she didn't like the side effects. The two things she hated the most were that medicine and the police. The police were the reason we replaced so many phones in that house. It was a shame. She would snatch those phones out of the wall in a minute. That really messed up my brother Joe, because he could stay on that phone three or four hours.

When our kids first came around Mom, they would run until they got used to her, but David's kids were older. They weren't scared of my mom. She never did bother those kids or talk crazy to them, but when she got sick my mom hated us at times, and she hated my dad the majority of the time.

My mom would go up the street to my Great Aunt Mert's house. As I said, my Aunt Mert was a school teacher. They would get in family arguments all the time and the next thing you know, my mom was upset and sick again. Aunt Mert would call my dad to come and get her before she could destroy her house.

Aunt Mert's two sons, Lawrence and John Heatley, were older than we were and they had two dogs, Frosty and Snowball. Those were soft names for attack dogs. I didn't like to go to their house because my cousin John would sic the dogs on me every time. John never did sic those dogs on my brothers, but I always had to sneak to get in their house because of those dogs.

My brother Marvel escaped a lot of the abuse from my mom because he moved to New York after college to pursue an acting career. Everybody was moving along with their lives. Their lifestyles changed as we got older and everyone seemed to be settling down—all except me. For some reason I just couldn't get it together. I was just a rebel. The lifestyle of a rebel took me into 35 years of drug addiction, four prison sentences, and five years of homelessness. I served a second prison term in 1986 at James Crabtree Correctional Center, then a third in 1991 at McAlester Work Release Center, and a fourth in 1994 in Woodward County, Oklahoma.

Because of who God is, something good came out of all that mess when I was converted to Jesus Christ and God began to speak to me about ministering to those who were living in the places I had been delivered from—prison and the streets.

As time went on and we all got older, the drama kept coming even though she was trying to slow herself down and keep herself out of the hospital. She was going to Eastern State Mental Hospital in Vinita, Oklahoma, in the 1970s through 1990s. Eastern State was about an hour and a half drive. The state closed down the mental institution in Taft. It is now part of a prison and minimum security prison.

My mom went to the hospital so much that the insurance ran out and they wouldn't accept her any more so we were on our own. We could only send her to the outpatient clinics and they didn't keep her any longer than two weeks, though it took longer than that for her to recover. After she got out, she would quickly return back to the hospital because she wouldn't be completely well.

When Aunt Mert passed away, my mom just couldn't take it. She was terrible at the funeral. She went off. The preacher was preaching and my mom started yelling, "Don't nobody want to hear no mother f_____ preaching. You mother f_____ better sing." You think we didn't? It sounded so bad because everybody was singing different songs. Some people were scared. The pastor finally got everyone on the same chorus. I was glad when that was over!

I knew one person who could calm down my mom, her great-nephew Guan. He was one of her favorite nephews on her side of the family. Music helped, too, because it relaxed her. If you were going to my mom's house and she was sick, if you got within two blocks of our house, you could hear music playing so loud you would have thought it was a block party.

One day we were driving up to my mom's and the door was wide open. When we pulled up and got out of the car, my mom and dad had been tussling, because my dad refused to let that demonic spirit destroy him and his kids.

When we went in the house, my mom had a heavy oak table in the air over her head. It had baffle glass on it that was about an inch thick. She had gotten mad for some reason and she picked up that coffee table from the middle of our living room floor and threw it down. That thing must have weighed at least a hundred pounds. She busted that table into so many pieces, you know what that meant. It was time to go. I told my Marya, "Let's go, Honey! We are out!"

There was never a dull moment because she would always say something crazy or do something crazy.

One time my mom and dad were arguing and she said, "You know what, Holloway? Your last name Johnson isn't
_____. Pretty soon they are going to stop making Johnson's baby powder." Where did she get that from?

Marya and I were cleaning new homes for a living and we were riding with my boss, Leon Curry, when a news break came on the radio saying that a woman had barricaded herself in a house. Next came the address: "The location is 1720 East Woodrow Street"

"Oh my God!" I said.

"What's wrong?" asked Leon.

"That's my mom."

"Quit playing."

"I'm serious. Take me to a pay phone." Cell phones weren't that popular back then.

I told Leon I had to go and check out what was going on and that the enemy was trying his best to destroy our family and bring division. However, I knew that one day we would have the victory.

One time Marya had to get a ride to pick up some money at Western Union. She called and asked my mom to take her. At that time she did not know the nature of my mom's illness as we did. That spirit would fool people, because she was like a baseball player. She threw a change-up and you could really be fooled, especially if you didn't know Jesus or didn't have God's discernment.

Many people came and picked up my mom at her house, but you were crazy if you let my mom drive and pick *you* up. Anyway, when I came in from work, before I could hardly get in the door, Marya said, "I am never getting in your mom's car again!" What had she done now? "Your mom was in downtown Tulsa driving down one-way streets, going on red, stopping on green, and people were blowing their horns, and she would just sit there! I tried to tell her that the light had changed and it was our time to go, and she went off. She said, "Don't try to tell me about these streets. I know these mother f_____ streets like the back of my hand. I've been here all my life. You just sit over there and ride." Marya was so shocked and in such a panic that she said she was scared to get out of the car. But I admire my wife for hanging in there with my mom.

Another time, we got *put* out of the car. We had been riding with my mom before this incident out north of the city. She went into her purse to look for some money. Marya and I got quiet and I thought to myself, "O Lord, I hope she finds it; please let her find it." I knew that if she didn't see her money, she was going to cause a problem and blame us for taking it, and that's exactly what happened. She asked, "Which one of you mother f_____ has got my money?"

We tried to explain that we didn't have it, but it wasn't working. She pulled that car over to the side of the road and I already had my hand on the door handle, ready to open that door. I knew what would be next and it was just what I expected. I didn't know whether she would go for a gun or a knife but it wasn't either one. It was a machete! That was way bigger than a knife.

She had the handle on that machete and was pulling that thing out from under that car seat, but before we could even see how long it was, and before she could tell us to get out, we were gone! We just happened to be in the neighborhood where our in-laws Ping and William lived. Later on that evening, things went from bad to extremely bad. She went through my dad's house with a baseball bat and for no reason knocked holes in all the hallway walls and bedroom doors, just because she got mad. Then the next Sunday at church she suddenly jumped up and ran straight out the door into traffic, where a 1977 Good Times van hit her and knocked her 300 feet down the street. My dad, the pastors, brothers, and saints came out of the church and ran down to where she was lying in the middle of the street and started praying for her.

All of a sudden, she rose up like in the movie *The Exorcist* and said in a very deep possessed voice to my dad, and the others, "Get your mother f_____ hands off me! I don't want anybody praying for me but David."

My dad told me what had happened. My nephew Mario Harris saw it all. I wasn't there but if I had heard that kind of voice I would probably have taken off because I wasn't saved yet and I didn't have any power over those demonic spirits. I would probably have been so high at that time that I would have wacked out and taken off running. All you would have seen of Alvin would have been a cartoon of my elbows and the bottom of my feet. As tough as I thought I was back then, I wasn't going to be messing with a demon. But now? I'll cast one out in a minute.

My dad said that when the paramedics came on the scene she jumped straight up off the street. They talked her into going to the hospital to get checked out but all she suffered was a broken wrist. But that demon kept on attacking our family and my dad. My mom's mind and body were being used by that demon. What's going to be next?

CHAPTER 5.

AMAZING EXAMPLE OF A GODLY DAD

When I was eight years old, I was a little kid at a revival with my dad when I saw the Holy Ghost move for the first time in my life. When the Holy Spirit hit my dad, he started spinning like a top in the middle of the floor. I will never forget it. He came up speaking in tongues, crying, and praising God and that scared me because at eight years old I didn't know what was happening. Later I learned that's where he got his strength.

After he was saved my dad was always in church and he brought us up to always be in church, , too, whether we liked it or not. It was never our decision, only his. We always read through the Bible with my dad and he taught us about demonic spirits. I guess that was because we were dealing with one in our own home.

Telling my dad that you didn't want to go to church was unacceptable and any of our friends who stayed all night with us knew enough to bring their church clothes. We were members at Northside Church of God in Christ (COGIC).

There was Sunday School at 9:00 AM, regular service at 11:00 AM, which usually lasted till 3:00 PM or 4:30 PM, and then back at 6:00 PM for YPWW (Young People Willing and Working), and then night service at 8:00 PM. We wouldn't get out of service until 11:00 PM or midnight, and after everybody got through fellowshipping, it would be 12:30 AM or 1:00 AM when we got home. Dad was not worried about us going to school that next morning. He had God and serving Jesus on his mind.

As I said earlier, my brothers and I had to read the Scriptures and tell Dad what they meant and we always had to take turns leading prayer. Dad was like this: "As long as you are under this roof, you will serve the Lord in this house." He didn't compromise.

One Sunday in the 1990s, Mom was on a roll again. She came to the church where my brother Marvel was preaching. He was boasting about how the Lord had allowed him to be able to bless the pastor of the church with a thousand dollars for his anniversary.

What did he say that for? My mom stood up in the church and she said, "Negro, you did what? How in the hell can you give your pastor a thousand dollars, Negro, when your _____ owes me seven hundred?" The church got quiet, and you should have seen my brother's face.

My dad tried to play it off. He just started giggling, and my momma said, "What the hell are you laughing at with those three teeth hanging out of your mouth?"

I wasn't embarrassed. What for? I was used to it by now.

One time she came walking in the church door with a cup of wine in her hand and one of the ushers tried to stop her. One of Marvel's in-laws, William, told that usher who didn't know my mom to just leave her alone because he knew it would be a disaster approaching hear about that cup of wine. She went right in the church and sat down.

William and his wife Helen "Ping" Hudson had known my mom for years. Their mother, Momma Cotton, was a friend of our family and we all attended the same church.

My mom respected my dad for raising us up in church, but when that wrong spirit invaded her soul that was the last thing on her mind. When that happened, often times my dad was her target.

One time my mom tried to put some of her medicine into my dad's juice that he always kept in the refrigerator to stay cold, but men of God have a discerning spirit at times. He said he knew his drink wasn't right as soon as he picked it up.

My mom said she did it because she wanted him to know how it felt to take that medicine and wanted him to feel the side effects it had on her.

When I think about my mom, I think about Ephesians 6:12 (KJV): *"For we wrestle not against flesh and blood, but against principalities, against powers against the rulers of the darkness of this world, and against spiritual wickedness in high places."*

When I think about my dad, I think about Isaiah. 54:17 (KJV): *"No weapon that is formed against me shall prosper, and every tongue that shall rise against thee in judgment thou shall condemn."*

My dad taught us so well about the ways of God that even during the years that I strayed away, his teachings never left me. I was just on the back side of the mountain for a while, getting prepared, and God was positioning me for a time such as this when I would live for Christ.

My dad lived out his faith in a godly manner. He laid a foundation in our lives that was reality to him. It was solid, not one bit counterfeit.

As it says in 1 Corinthians 3:11 (KJV), *". . . for other foundation can no man lay than that is laid, which is Jesus Christ."*

Dad always said, "I'm that tree planted by the water that shall not be moved, and nothing will ever separate me from the love of God."

I guess my mom had raised so much hell that my dad said he wasn't going to live in hell on earth and then waste his life, die and go to hell, and neither were his children.

He prayed every one of us through, and I'm praying that for my whole family.

My dad was a humble man, and sometimes when my mom was sick she would say that Holloway wasn't our daddy, but we knew better.

My mom would bring men over to our house and my dad would never argue with those men. He always spoke and kept on going. My mom would always say that they were her friends, but we wanted to beat on all of them.

We didn't play when it came to respect for my dad because he was so good to us. We never heard my dad curse, or lie intentionally, or cheat, steal, commit adultery, mistreat anybody, or argue with them, or do anything out of character. He really was good to my mom, considering the circumstances.

My dad always said that if anybody ever messed with his kids, he was going to step out of church for a minute and handle his business with that person, and he was serious.

I got in trouble at school a lot and was suspended about once every year. For some reason I always hung out with the wrong crowd, like gang members. I also had followers. I was the class clown and I got the most whippings.

I always ran with older crowds because they told good exciting stories, and some told good lies. The older ones also got me drinking wine and smoking as a young boy. If my dad had found out he probably would have stepped out of church and killed every one of them.

One night we were hanging out down the street with the other kids on the block and it started to get dark. Joe and I weren't as old as David and Marvel, so we started heading for the house.

"Where are you all going?" David asked.

"Home! You know it's getting late. It's about 10:30 and you know how Daddy is."

"You all can hang out here with us tonight, and I'll tell Daddy you all were here with me."

"OK."

We got to talking and having fun, and before we realized, it was 1:30 AM in the morning. "We know we're in trouble," we told David.

David said, "Well I didn't tell you all to stay out this late."

We all shouted, "Liar!"

As we started walking home headed to the top of the hill towards the dead end, all I could think about was that big long switch that dad had in his bedroom behind that door. That seemed like the longest walk of my life at that time.

Finally, we were at the house hoping that maybe Daddy was asleep. After easing the door open, we crept in the house, tipping on our toes, one by one. All of a sudden that door slammed, and we knew it wasn't from one of us or the wind, because we weren't making any noise, and the wind wasn't blowing. Out of nowhere sudden a switch about six feet long hit every one of us at the same time! We started yelling that David had said it was all right. The whole time my dad was beating us, he was asking, "Is David your daddy? Is David your daddy" We didn't ever trust David again.

My dad's faith in God really brought us through even though Momma brought so much hurt and pain to our family. I didn't know if we would ever recover, but we did, so I know it wasn't anybody but God. God did it and God brought us through. There's no doubt in my mind that God is real. I have to keep addressing that because it is true.

God has put us under submission to people in authority. That's called leadership. You don't go against your brothers and your sisters. If you can't submit to leadership or to another person whom God has put in charge over you, you can't submit to God.

I almost got caught up in the wrong attitudes toward leaders when I first got saved until I learned that the devil will trick you to go against them. Then the Lord opened my eyes. Psalm 119:18 says (paraphrased), *"Open my eyes, Lord, and show me wondrous things of thy law."*

Jesus said if there is any unforgiveness in your heart, you will not see the Kingdom of Heaven. He said that in the same way as he has forgiven you, you must also forgive.

My dad said that whatever situation people are going through to pray for them but guard your own heart. Everybody may not be on your level. Do what God wants *you* to do but let *them* take their matters up with God.

Don't go to hell because of your reaction to someone else's tribulation. Be kind to them, but don't let them get you off course. Pray for them, but don't let them get you out of your relationship with God.

What if Jesus returned for you while you were in sin because of a bad attitude in a relationship? You might not have time to repent.

The Bible said Jesus will return to this earth in the twinkling of an eye, and you can't get *"Lord, I repent"* out of your mouth that quick.

Stay in God's will and live for His purposes and not yours, because it's not about us. It's about HIM (Him In Me). Remember, God is ultimately in control, but he often works indirectly through others.

My dad had a big pastor's heart. He respected everybody he came in contact with. He gave out food baskets every year to the destitute. To me, he wasn't only my dad but also a true man of God, holy, sanctified, and a man of honor, standards, principles, character, and integrity.

Most of all, I saw humility in his life. My dad had hopes for everyone. As the Scripture says in 1 John 3:3, *"Every man that has hope in him purifieth himself, even as he is pure."*

My dad's life before God set the best example for us of how to be a good father. The best thing that could happen to any child is to have a father who lives for the Lord and to receive the Holy Spirit who guides us into all truth.

We boys were blessed with the right fruit that fell off the right tree. My dad left us a bite of that fruit that let me taste the goodness of the Lord in the land of the living.

We went through so much as kids that words can't describe it. My mom could have killed any one of us at any time, but my dad's prayers were sincere and they were answered because of the marriage covenant he made with my mom before the Lord.

I believe that my dad's prayers saved our lives till this day, not only from my mom, but from hell, and the hell that was in our home. My dad believed in the Lord's promises, Yea and Amen. The prayers of the righteous man availed much, and also the prayers of relatives and friends.

I had experiences in life that gave me compassion and understanding that I believe can help the culture.

Those experiences included some violent interactions with the police, but not the kind you might expect.

CHAPTER 6.

MOM ROUGHS UP THE POLICE

I remember one time back in the 1980s when I was about 11 years old and my dad tried to be slick and call the police because my mom was getting out of control again. She heard him make the call but didn't say a word. My mother went in the kitchen and started boiling water in a huge pot. I thought she was preparing to cook some greens. As the police were on their way, she was sitting in the living room on the couch and she told me to sit down beside her.

She said that when I heard a knock on the door she was going to count to three, and then I should open the door. I started thinking about what she had said and then something just snapped in me. I thought about Daddy and that phone call to the police.

All of a sudden, we heard the knock and she told me, "Go to the door, but don't open it until I tell you." She got up off the couch and went in the kitchen, and when she came out of that kitchen she had a huge pot of boiling water and she was counting, "One, two, three, open the door!" As the police started to step in the door, my mom told me to get back, and she let them have it!

When that hot water hit them, they took off running and screaming and she slammed that door and locked it. The police left and didn't come back and dad and I left and didn't come back, either. My mom knew my dad had called the police on her and he knew he would be her next target. That's why we left—we went into our survival mode.

Sometimes when my brothers were hanging out in the street, I would go stay at friends' houses or with my relatives. One time in the middle 1980s we got a call from one of my mother's friends that we had better get over to the Car Wash Club on Pine Street, because my mom was over there shooting up the place. My brother and dad rushed over there and I came later. It was about 10:00 PM when this incident happened and everybody in the restaurant was on the floor. My dad and brother got there just in time because the police already had their guns drawn on my mother and were ready to shoot her. My dad and David jumped out of the car yelling, "Don't shoot! Don't shoot! She's a mental patient!"

The angels had protected my mom as usual. After that I guess my dad and brother talked her into putting down the gun because she wasn't listening to the police at all. She just kept reloading. When I got there, so many bullet holes were in the front of the building. Thank God no one was shot or injured. We were truly blessed on that call, and all we could hear was my dad saying, "Thank you Lord, in the name of Jesus!"

We also heard people saying things like, "That's Maxine. I guess she had one of her fits," or "Somebody made her mad," or "She's just crazy."

We got calls about my mom all the time and people used to laugh at her because they didn't understand her condition. My dad had already programmed us not to let it bother us and we didn't at times, but you wanted to bust people in the head when they were talking about your mom. You know, at one time you would get knocked out for talking about someone's mother.

We had to call the police to help us a lot because you couldn't handle my mom one-on-one when she was sick. I don't care who you were, not unless you had help from the Lord, because it took my dad and all my brothers to get my mom on the ground.

One time we tied my mom up with some torn up sheets to restrain her until the police got there, though it was hard to get them to come back out to our house. She was on the warpath for real that time and she was destroying everything in sight in our house like a human tornado. When the police got there, they put handcuffs on my mom while she was still tied up in those sheets. When we got my mom to her feet she started cursing and calling us all kinds of names.

She said the Lord told her to break out of the handcuffs and she did! We had a scene in our front yard. People were looking and laughing but they also knew what to do when she broke out of those handcuffs. Run!

You didn't have to tell the police. They had already made their move. The Tulsa Police had come to know my mom very well, and I mean on a first-name basis. They remembered that address that is the title of this book, 1720 East Woodrow Street, because of the hot-water incident. They were the first to leave, just like us. By the time we returned that night, mom was exhausted and we were able to get her to the hospital. We never could get the police to come back to our house again and I don't know to this day what happened to those handcuffs.

My momma's oldest sister, Thelma, ran clubs, laundromats, pool halls, and liquor stores. She sold bootleg liquor on Greenwood Street. But my mother never drank alcohol or went to clubs until she got sick.

One day she was down the street at a club called Flags, a bootleg joint where people bought liquor on Sunday when the liquor store was closed. She was shooting pool and a man tried to go into her purse. She caught him and a struggle broke out.

He hit my mom in the chin with a pool stick and busted it wide open. What did he do that for? She stabbed him repeatedly. The man had been warned earlier by Leroy, one of our friends, but I guess he didn't hear very well or didn't care, but eventually he really got the point.

When the man tried to take my dad to court to pay for his medical bills, they dismissed it because the man brought that on himself.

By the way, since I mentioned Leroy, once Leroy had our car in his mechanic shop and was taking too long to fix it, so we had to borrow my mother's car. She was sick and started acting crazy when we asked to borrow the car. After a week she wanted her car back. I told her that Leroy wasn't working on the car and he always had an excuse, but his price was better than all the other shops.

Early one morning we were riding with some friends and we passed his shop before it opened. Then I just realized that guess who? Mother was at Leroy's shop. All kinds of thoughts ran through my head because mom was sitting in the driveway reading a newspaper. Oh, my God!

We didn't hear anything drastic that evening, but he called the next day and told us the car was ready. He didn't have to say anything. We knew Maxine Johnson was behind it.

You see, we knew our mom would attack us with cast iron skillets, pots and pans, a knife, or a gun. She would try anything, but we quickly got it right. My dad knew we could take care of ourselves when we grew up because we had plenty of combat training, as we called it.

When I was in tenth grade I had to have a hernia operation and two or three days after my surgery my mom came to the hospital at 3:00 AM. I could hear the doctors telling her she couldn't see me. I was asleep until I heard the commotion that woke me up. The first thing I thought was "Momma!"

I could barely get up but when I stepped into the hallway all I could see was a doctor's coattail flying. My mom had picked him up and thrown him through a picture window. Security came and they took my mom to the psych ward on the ninth floor. Everyone in the hospital was shocked, but not me. It didn't bother me or surprise me one bit, because I had been living it half of my life.

But you know, after all that we saw and talked about, when my mother wasn't sick the police and my neighbors and a lot of others had total respect for my mom. Nobody said anything bad about her then and most people who were close to us really understood.

One day we got a call from the neighbors saying that a man on the next street over had a shotgun on my mother because she was sitting on his porch, deranged and lost, and had forgotten where she lived. When we got there, he had already called the police. We explained the problem before the police got there and he put down the shotgun.

When the police arrived, Mom asked them, "Why are you here?" They already knew my mom and one policeman knew me, because he had arrested me before.

Mom asked the police, "Why are you taking me? He's the pot smoker," talking about me. Marya started laughing and I tried to laugh and play it off, too. My mom was the one they should have worried about because she had destroyed so many of their police cars, but this time she went along without combat. Once again, "Thank you Jesus."

Pastor David Brandon, my brother in Christ and a former NFL football player and great friend with whom I have the pleasure of serving in prison ministry, said, "You can look back and see God's handprint on all of it."

We were always on a survival mission when those moments occurred. There was a lot of laughter, abuse, hurt, and heartache, suicidal thoughts, pain, and challenges, stress, depression, embarrassment, you name it, but in the midst of all of that you just had to keep a sense of humor.

My mom and dad could be very comical in some of those moments. You can't tell me that laughter isn't good for the soul.

One time my mom had to be taken off the airplane in Dallas, Texas, on an emergency landing, because of a mental breakdown she had on the plane coming back from San Francisco, where she had attended her sister's funeral. They took my mom off the plane and rushed her to a mental hospital in Dallas. My aunt said that one of the things that happened on the plane was that my mom tried to get in the cockpit. She was talking about she can fly this mother f_____ airplane. Two weeks later my dad and brother had to go to Dallas and pick her up. I'm glad I didn't make that trip. As my dad would have said, "Thank You, Jesus!"

When my mom was 65 years old she was at her friend's bootlegger joint when her friend called us to hurry over because she said it looked like she was going to act up. That house joint was right around the corner from my oldest brother David's house. The neighbors had already called the police before we even got there and a policewoman had already arrived by herself.

The homeowner directed us to the back of the house because my mom had tried to get away out the back door and the policewoman had gone after her. If she knew what I knew, she would have let her keep running.

When we got in the back, my mom and her friend Mary Ann had that police woman on the ground beating her. Mary Ann is the mother of one of my play sisters, Eunice Thompson, and Mary Ann just happened to be over at the joint with her. When we got there, we pulled them off the police officer and when that officer got up she was ready to run, gun and all. I think she forgot that she was the police and had a gun the way she took off.

When other officers came they couldn't find my mom. Of course, they already knew her. "I see you met Maxine," they said to the female officer.

"You know her?" she asked them.

"We have been dealing with Maxine for years."

"How are you doing, Rev," the officer said to my dad. "We meet again, I see."

"Next time I get a call on her I will let someone else get that call," the lady officer replied, and I thought in my mind, *Oh, that call is coming, but I just don't know when.*

My mom had taken off running and had hurdled two four-foot fences heading toward my brother's house. We didn't say anything to the police but we knew that's where we would find her. When we got to my brother's house, she was sitting on my brother's porch smoking a cigarette as if nothing had ever happened. She was switch-hitting again, and the police didn't try to find her. As a matter of fact, they didn't do anything to her or her friend Mary Ann. I guess they forgot about it and didn't want to deal with that situation. After all the commotion, we all told my mom that she was really getting too old for this, but she didn't say a word. It was as if we weren't even there.

We really found out about trusting in the Lord because our lives were always on the line. You didn't know at times if you were even going to see tomorrow, except that you were taught to trust in the Lord at an early age. We would ask, Why us? Why my parents? Why is this happening to us?

And then dad would say, "You don't question God."

"Well, what do you do?"

His response was always, "You just pray, son, you just pray." And you know what? He was right. You just pray and in the long run you will find out at an early age, or at an older age, that God truly does answer prayers. That's why I'm still alive today to let you know that prayer works.

CHAPTER 7.

HOW MY DAD WON HIS RACE

I begin to cry sometimes when I think about my childhood, especially when I see someone going through some of the same things I did. My heart goes out to them because I know it's a struggle.

My dad is the reason all of us boys are now strong men. He's the reason I eventually stopped being a rebel and became a minister of the Lord.

I remember my dad telling me about how he came to the Lord. He said one night he was drinking and driving drunk down Riverside Drive in Tulsa when he apparently passed out and fell asleep at the wheel of his car. The car went off the shoulder of the road and ended up in the Arkansas River.

As Dad came to, he had an encounter with Jesus that changed his whole life. While he was facing a life-and-death moment, he made a covenant with the Lord.

I could hear my dad saying to the Lord, "If you just give me a second chance at life, no matter what becomes of me, I will be sold out for you."

The only book I ever saw my dad read was the Bible. He never wanted anything but God's best for us. When you ignore your parents, sometimes you bring tribulation on yourself just as I did, but when you have a strong dad who is saved the Lord does miracles through him.

My dad made us strong kids, even though some of the abuse we took from my mom at an early age scarred all of us. The scars will never leave because they are permanent, but the Lord healed those wounds.

Overall, we were there for my mom and so were others. She didn't know any better, as my dad would always say. "Baby, she's just sick, and one day you will understand."

God let us go through that lifestyle because it was meant for the development of the Johnson boys at 1720 East Woodrow Street. I know that one of my brothers is still suffering from it, but my dad got the whole package because he was the head of the household. He stayed on his knees and he was always at revivals and in church, and he never gave up.

My dad had all of us in those revivals right along with him, up all night. Eventually, he won the race to bring his sons along with him into the Kingdom of God. My dad prophesied that before he passed away all his kids would become ordained ministers or pastors, and in 2004, before my dad's death, I was the last one to come into the ministry. And so his prophecy was manifested. Today every one of us is saved and in ministry.

When I gave my life to Christ, I tried to make up for so much wrong and hurt I had caused him when I was in rebellion in the world. How did I go wrong and end up the wrong way? The devil was really after me to do a devil's job—kill, steal, and destroy—because he knew there was a calling on my life.

When you have a life that's predestinated to fulfill God's will, you can only run so far because whatever sin or lifestyle you are in when God chooses you, it's over. Remember, that's all that came out of my mouth. *"It's over."*

My dad passed away at the age of 84 in 2005 just as I started writing this story. I happened to be there at my 25th class reunion and I went to his house to visit him. I had just left his house to get on the highway and return to Atlanta. I was approaching Broken Arrow, Oklahoma, when my brother David said, "Turn back around."

I said, "For what?"

He said, "Dad just passed away."

So I turned around and headed back to my dad's house. He had been moved from the living room into the bedroom and when I went in the bedroom I could feel the presence of the Holy Spirit. I believe that the angels of the Lord came and took him away. A power came over my body that I had never felt before. I knew that his work was finished here on earth.

My dad most definitely won the race and won the fight thanks to a God who never did forsake him or give up on him. I know that the Lord said to him, "Well done, Holloway, well done." He won that fight against an assigned demonic spirit (or legions of them) that controlled my mom at times and worked through her to try to keep him out of God's will. He never submitted to that evil spirit. He was an awesome man of God.

Looking back through the eyes of a child and then through the eyes of a man, I know I inherited his traits and that's why I can praise God and bless him right now. If God never does anything else for me again, he's done enough.

If we learned nothing else from my parents, they taught us how to love unconditionally. Momma was good as gold when that demon wasn't attacking her. Even though she went through that ordeal, she still won at the end because she gave her life to the one who was really after her, Jesus. It's never about how you start, but it's about how you finish.

What are you going to do when Jesus chooses you? I just wanted to be obedient to God, as my dad was. However, it was not just because of who my dad was but because of who

Jesus is. God requires obedience from us because the Bible says obedience is better than sacrifice.

You can experience everything you see and get everything you desire, but it will never be enough to satisfy you.

I found out that there is a place that's located in your heart that only Jesus can fill. That's why I finally returned to God at an older age, because my dad taught me that God can't lie and his Word says if you give your life to him he will save you and your family.

Of all the bloodshed I saw in our dysfunctional family, the only blood that counted was the blood of Jesus. I experienced the fruit of the Spirit like love, joy, and peace only after I was transformed and started to become like Christ. The lusts of the flesh profited me nothing.

The Lord blessed my dad in his obedience, but the opposite is also true. The Bible says disobedience is just like witchcraft. "For rebellion is as the sin of witchcraft, and stubbornness is as iniquity and idolatry" (1 Samuel 15:23 KJV).

The devil really thought he had me in my disobedience, but thanks to the prayers of a righteous man, God showed me a different plan.

Just in time, I defeated the devils in my life and my dad was able to celebrate my victory in Christ before he went home to the Lord.

CHAPTER 8.

DEFEATING THE DEVILS IN MY LIFE

I have been through so much in my life that it's amazing I am still alive and saved. The devil was working overtime.

I was a gang-banger

Involved in shoot-outs

Pimped women

Went to prison four times

Was hit on a motorcycle going 65 miles an hour without breaking speed

Drove my car and hit a little boy when I was strung out on PCP, almost killing him

Was thrown out of the car thirty feet, and came out without a scratch

Had a loaded gun pointed at my head and they kept clicking the trigger and it didn't go off, so they let me go

Was a crack-addict for 25 years, and an addict for 35

Shot-up heroin a couple of times

Shot up plenty of cocaine, dipped rocks of cocaine into PCP and let them dry, and smoked them. We called it space-basing.

Had just about every kind of acid and pills. You name it, I have just about done it.

I have been on drugs more of my life that I have been clean.

When I first became on fire for the Lord, here comes the devil again. I had started serving and cleaning the church but one day while I was cleaning I got sick, so I went to get checked out. I was diagnosed with hepatitis C. My liver was failing me.

My faith level had to rise because I was challenged with trusting the Lord again as a rededicated Christian. I had to drive out fear and sickness with faith and belief and God would come through for me.

It turned out that it was no challenge for God after the encounter I had with Jesus. I knew God would restore me and after I went through treatment for six months I was totally delivered and I am healed from hepatitis C to this day.

Sometime later a deadly spirit of cancer came on me. In August 2010 I was on a church outing at Holcomb Bridge Recreation Park and really having fun. We had one of those married couples' challenges, a race where you and your spouse's legs are tied together and you have to race to the finish line.

While racing with my wife, I fell on my side and she fell on top of me, but we got up and everything seemed fine and I really just shook it off. However, on Monday when I went to clean the church I pulled up in the parking lot and suddenly I was spitting up bright red blood. It stopped but later on that evening I ended up going to the emergency room at Emory Johns Creek hospital. They told me it was just a sinus issue and sent me home.

A month later, I was at home brushing my teeth when all of a sudden here comes a big clot of blood out of my mouth again, so back to the emergency room for round two.

"Well, Mr. Johnson, we checked you over and everything seems all right." Okay, maybe it's just those old nosebleeds I use to have when I was little. So I left again. A month later it happened for the third time. Here we go again.

I took a picture of this bright red blob of blood in the sink and went back to the emergency room, but this time I was not leaving until I had an answer. A nurse came in and said, "I'm going to be your angel today, Mr. Johnson," and my response to her was, "I really need one about now."

She said she was going to send me to an ear, nose, and throat doctor so I could get checked out from the neck up because most of the time doctors check the lower part of your body.

When I went to the ear, nose, and throat doctor they said that I had to get a biopsy on my throat, so they scheduled me for a week later. When I went to that appointment they found a tumor at the base of my tongue. The doctor told my wife that information privately because he wanted her to tell me after I had awakened from the anesthesia, but she waited until I got home to tell me.

I can remember it just as though it were yesterday. When we got home I laid down to rest and she came in the room and said, "I have to tell you something." I already knew from God's discernment what she was going to say.

When she told me that I had cancer, I broke out laughing! She was sitting there crying but I had already declared my healing in advance. It was only the latest demon on the list trying to stop me from serving Jesus. Why wouldn't I break out laughing?

When we went back to the doctor, I asked him, "How long have I had cancer?" He told me it had probably started about three years earlier. I asked him what stage I was in and he told me I was in the latter part of stage four.

I knew it would take all of my faith and belief in God to bring me through. But after 46 treatments of chemotherapy and 46 treatments of radiation, God brought me through in spite of a 30 percent survival rate for a person my age (54) at stage four.

Those treatments had a dramatic effect on my life.

After the first two weeks of chemo and radiation my weight dropped from 235 pounds to 140 pounds. It was the most devastating physical experience of my life.

Sometime later, cancer returned to my thyroid and my lymph nodes and for a while it seemed like surgery after surgery, but God is still faithful so I actually beat cancer three times. Glory to God!

Right until this day I am cancer-free and all glory goes to God Almighty. I am strong and back in the ministry and the Lord is moving strongly in my life again. I'm back pounding in the prisons again and I'm traveling the roads all over Georgia.

God is a great God! Sometimes that's all I can say. I have to thank him every day.

When I look back at my challenges and my struggles, my heart just hurts until I say, "Thank you, Lord, for being there for me, even when I didn't acknowledge you in my time of need, and I mean that from my heart."

I'm so thankful to the Lord for adopting me into his family and giving me his spiritual DNA.

The world didn't care about me. People in sin eventually showed me what they were all about. They were not real friends. *But Jesus! You are truly a Friend to me!*

I love the way the Lord takes the most messed up people and uses them for testimonies for Christ and to be a witness for him and to use us for his glory. That's my story. I least deserved it but God became my dad and made me his child and now he takes care of me.

"The spirit bears witness with our spirit that we are children of God" (Romans 8:16 KJV).

Jesus said tribulations will come. Do you think Jesus, God's Son, went through all of his mess for us and we don't have to go through anything in his family? If you think that, you have lost your mind.

I learned that the right thing to do is to trust God and forever keep learning more ways to live a godly life according to Scripture, because it's the best life you could ever have. It's a challenge, but it's a peaceful one.

Even though you still go through things, it is much better than drugs, robbing, shooting, arguing, fighting, stealing, cheating, sex sin, partying all night, and hanging in the streets all night looking for trouble.

Sometimes I have said all I want to a person about knowing Jesus or being saved by believing in Jesus, but they wouldn't take heed until they faced a life-threatening situation. Even then they might take heed only for a moment. Later on in life they forget about him because they are, as Momma Katheryn Boone puts it, "Saved for a moment"—just long enough for God to get them out of trouble or save them from some illness or death. After that, they still turn their back on him again. That's what I did so many times.

God is there for more than a moment, even when you forget who really delivered and saved you. He protected me when I was in prison all four times, but when I got out, it was only a moment before I said, "God who?"

I admit that I was wrong as a father and I've asked God to forgive me. Even though my dad was the best example of a dad I could have had, I wish I had been a better dad years ago, setting an example for my youngest son Alonzo, whom I spoke about, who probably would have been alive today if I had taught my sons God's way instead of the world's way.

Even though I grew up in church, I went away from God and had to learn things by tribulation, not by revelation. I paid dearly for a lack of wisdom. It's not my dad's fault, because I was taught the right way. I take responsibility for my own life, as we all should. We will be held accountable by God for our lifestyles.

I can reflect back to my childhood days when my dad spoke about these things that are taking place right now in this generation. He taught us that judgment is coming. The older I get, the more I tell people when I am witnessing to them, beware because you are either getting closer to heaven or hell. Oh! I know that's a Selah, if you are a believer.

Here it is, years later, and I'm living strong for the Lord. God has blessed me to be able to launch my own prison ministry called Lethal Weapon Prison Ministries. I'm hitting prisons in the State of Georgia and I'm also a member of Prison Fellowship International.

God is moving in my life and I'm moving with him into all the places I can find where those demons who attacked me still hide out to steal, kill, and destroy others.

When I go out to the prisons to preach, everyone who comes with me is amazed to see how many of those who listen to me are broken down, crying, giving their lives to the Lord, just as I did.

If you don't see God moving, you must be standing still. I'm moving out, witnessing everywhere I can and every place that God is ordering my steps. I visit the adult prison systems, juvenile detention centers, county jails, group homes. I work with at-risk kids.

We might not admit it, but all of us have some family member or friend who is incarcerated, even if it's only a bondage in their mind. As Christians we cannot look at them any different from the way we want people to look at us. Anybody can get trapped or caught up, whether you are saved or not. One thing that I do know is that the church did not embrace me when I got out of prison.

Some Christians will look at you up side your head sideways. But the truth may be that when they were in the world they probably had done so much out there that they should have been to prison. But God just had his grace and mercy on them. That's why we have to judge ourselves first. Then we have to be careful whom we judge and how we judge them because the Lord will turn that back on us!

The Word says, *"For if we would judge ourselves, we should not be judged"* (1 Corinthians 11:31 KJV).

Jesus said, *"The standard you use in judging is the standard by which you will be judged"* (Matthew 7:2 NLT).

When I got saved, I remember saying, I don't want to be around all these fake preachers. And then the voice of the Lord said, "Then show me what the real thing looks like."

Some of your friends don't believe that you are a man of God now. Some will respect you and some won't. You will face challenges such as losing friends when you start living for the Lord but I guess it's because they have seen so much of your bad side that they don't think you could have a good side. However, always remember that there's some good in everybody and most of the time after you are changed by the Lord you really do more good than bad.

The Bible says that *"If any man be in Christ he is a new creature, old things passed away, behold all things become new"* (2 Corinthians 5:17), so I'm not that person that I was before in the world. The old Alvin is dead. You will never see him again, God willing, even though at times some people and situations will try to make that old man rise up again in my life while I am trying to live holy and righteous.

I used to love the world and the material things in it, but the Lord says in Luke 9:25: *"What is a man advantaged, if he gain the whole world, and lose himself, or be cast away?"* You must put forth effort to walk toward God, because if you walk away from him, you don't want him.

I discovered that when you give your life to Christ, He will work out your problems. God doesn't just meet you halfway. He takes you all the way, even if you are facing the sudden death of someone you love.

The first funeral where I ever had to speak as a minister was for my own son Shay. It was a great challenge, but God gave me the strength and favor. This is how it happened.

Our ministry had scheduled a Kingmaker's Conference in Raleigh, North Carolina, and I attended the conference to take my wife and also to serve Bishop Wellington Boone. It was packed with 250 women and Bishop Boone prophesied over every woman at the conference. It took hours.

The whole time I stood beside him assisting him with the anointing oil and holding a bottle of drinking water I was receiving the residue from every prophecy. However, at the same time my phone was blowing up and I couldn't stop what I was doing to answer it.

After about two hours, Bishop Boone came to the end of the line so I took a peek at my phone. I had 22 missed calls. I just knew with that many calls back-to-back like that something wasn't right.

I was afraid to answer those calls but I finally built up my nerve. I seriously thought that something had happened to my brother Joe because he sometimes disappeared for months at a time. However, that wasn't it.

They asked me if I was sitting down, and I said yes. They said it was about Alvin "Shay," my oldest and my only son who was still living. Then that same voice from the past that told me when my youngest son died said that Shay had just been killed. One of his so-called friends had walked up to him when he was unarmed and shot him three times at close range in the chest with a nine millimeter gun.

I said, "This can't be happening!" Just two weeks earlier I had led Shay to the Lord. He was my only son! Kids are supposed to bury their parents. We are not supposed to bury them. The only thing I could do was look to the Lord. It was April 20, 2012.

Two other young people were killed that day and I knew them, too. What set my heart straight was knowing that before he got killed my son had apologized to me for all the pain and hurt that he had caused me and asked me to forgive him for disrespecting me in the past. That was two weeks before his death.

Prior to that, Shay had said to me that he wasn't going to live that long. As a matter of fact, he said he wasn't going to live past two weeks, and right on the money, two weeks later he was killed, and that's why he wanted to get it right.

It's amazing how God works. That's why my heart is at ease with his death and I know I will see my sons again as long as I continue to live strong for the Lord.

I believe that both of my sons knew the Lord but I can't lie. Sometimes I wonder about my youngest son's death. I believe in my heart that he had a chance to repent and ask

God's for forgiveness. Shouldn't that be every dad's heart for his child? You want to know that they made it in.

My youngest son Alonzo was also murdered. He was shot twice in the head and seven times in the chest with a sawed-off shotgun and brutally beaten up so badly you could hardly recognize him.

A friend of mine who was at the lake fishing heard the shots and went to the location. He knew that was my son, so he contacted the family.

Since I wasn't saved at that time, all I had on my mind was revenge and killing. We left Atlanta and drove to Tulsa. As soon as I got there, I tried to find out the details.

I was meeting with gang leaders and was ready to call shots. We tried to catch up with the killers, but as soon as we got to one place, they had just left to go to another. That happened repeatedly. It wasn't anything but the hand of God keeping that blood off my hands Now I understand that God had another plan and purpose for me.

People always say that they can imagine how I feel, but they really don't know. It hurts so bad sometimes when you hear people talk about their kids and how proud they are of them, and you know both of your kids were murdered.

It takes every bit of God to help me daily, but whatever we go through in life, God is still on the throne.

CHAPTER 9

WHAT GOD HATH JOINED TOGETHER

"What therefore God hath joined together, let not man put asunder" (Mark 10:9 KJV).

In 1997, not long before my mother passed away, my mom sneaked up on my dad when he was asleep and hit him on the head with a piece of iron for no reason at all and busted dad's head wide open. He called my brother David, who took him to the hospital.

We told my dad that this should be the final warning. He needed to move her out and get on with his life. However, my dad's response was, "I can't, because I stand on the Word of God, and the Lord said what God has joined together let no man put asunder."

What can you say about a man who stands on the Word as strongly as that? Receive it and apply it to your life. I really didn't understand it then. I know that if your life is in danger, or there is a case of adultery, you are permitted to divorce. His life was in danger from the beginning as far as I saw it, but he never took a way out. My dad really did trust in God to protect him. He wasn't just trying God. He really trusted him.

All of my brothers and I tried to get my dad to admit my mom to the mental ward, or leave her, but he never did. Years after my mother's mental and medical conditions collided with one another and became worse, she was diagnosed with breast cancer. She was eventually bedridden. My dad and brothers kept her at home as long as they could. They finally had to admit her to a nursing home. He never gave up on my mother. Once you lose hope it's pretty much a done deal.

That's the key. Never give up! God never gives up on us. He is always pursuing us.

My mom passed away two days before her seventieth birthday. At her bedside, my dad asked if she would accept Jesus as her personal Savior, and she said, "Yeah."

Mom said the sinner's prayer and confessed her sins and asked God for forgiveness for everyone she had disrespected or hurt. Surely she will be in paradise with Jesus. That's what I believe in my heart, that she went on home to be with the Lord.

During more than 48 years of marriage and everything they went through, they never broke up, nor separated—not even one day. This is why I admire my dad so much. He was faithful to God and to his marriage.

In 1 Corinthians 7:14 the Bible says that the unbelieving wife is sanctified by the believing husband, and I truly believe that if it had been the other way around, my mother would have done the same.

My dad taught us to always respect our mom no matter what her condition was, and we always did respect her, and my dad. We never cursed or drank in front of my dad or mother as long as they were living, but these days the times are so different.

There are not many dads in the homes of our cities in these days and times. Sadly, most of the dads are in prison, or on drugs, or not setting godly examples for our young men.

A woman can't teach a boy how to be a man, so I challenge men to come back to their rightful place with God and then in the home.

I am a lot like my dad, they say, especially since I rededicated my life to the Lord. I am a God-pleaser, not a man-pleaser, and now whatever I eat, or drink, or do, I truly do it unto the Lord.

I appreciate everyone who was a part of the struggle of my family at 1720 East Woodrow Street. Not only has God kept us, but he has kept us in his pavilion, in the secret place of his tabernacle where Momma's demons could not harm us, a place where he gave us rest.

REFLECTIONS.
WHAT THIS BOOK IS ALL ABOUT

This book is not about the Johnson family but about God. He allowed every one of us in my family to go through this so that our destiny in God would be fulfilled for his purposes. It was the way of the Johnson boys, set right in God's plan for his kingdom. What we do now we do for God.

When I meet people, I don't care how they look or what they've been through or what substances they've been taking. I explain to them about Jesus and what He did for me. I tell them my testimony and let them know that God's Word is real and it is reality to me. I ask them to accept my invitation to come to church, even if I have to pick them up and bring them, and when they do come, I let God do the changing.

When I invite people to church who don't know Christ, they can come to know him and his truth and can hear something that will change their lives.

If someone will not accept Jesus as their personal Savior, I ask them if there is any reason why. If they say no reason, I ask if they would like to, and if they say no again, that's when I let God use me at another level. I let the Holy Spirit take over.

We can't fix everything or everybody. Sometimes I might have to "shake the dust off my feet" when they keep resisting the truth. I have to move on because I know that I will not be received by everyone I come in contact with.

Some people have their own beliefs, but I'm always going to keep pounding the truth. The Word says, *"And they overcame him by the blood of the Lamb, and by the word of their testimony; and they loved not their lives unto the death"* (Revelation 12:11 *KJV).* I will stand on God's Word even if I get killed behind it. I would even lay down my life for what I believe. As I always say, I know God's glory will come out of my life.

Jesus has to be the center of a person's life. I don't know how people live without Jesus. He has become reality in my life and the only things that matter to me right now are the things that are eternal and permanent, fixed, uniform, and universal, because that's where it counts with God.

Tomorrow isn't promised to anyone. You know that, too. This is the only time in your life that you can get it right.

1720 East Woodrow Street was a life experience for us where only God could bring us through. I thank him every day and praise his name. Nobody gets the glory but God.

AUTHOR'S BIO.

Minister Alvin W. Johnson

Lethal Weapon
PRISON MINISTRIES

"Alvin Johnson is not only a prison evangelist. He is also a spiritual father. Men stay saved after they are released from prison because he continues to call them, confront them, and teach them how to live righteously, as God has taught him. He is the kind of Christian man we are all called to be."

BISHOP WELLINGTON BOONE
Chief Prelate, Fellowship of International Churches

MINISTER ALVIN W. JOHNSON serves as an ordained minister at The Father's House Church in Norcross, Georgia, under the leadership of Bishop Garland Hunt and Bishop Wellington Boone. He is the author of *1720 East Woodrow Street, The Alvin W. Johnson Story*, a book that details his miraculous transformation from failure into a minister of God.

In 2010, Minister Johnson founded Lethal Weapon Prison Ministries to minister to inmates and to assist released inmates to establish productive lives in society through Christ. He is a non-compromising preacher with a desire for the fruit of the Spirit to be evident in his life who is especially effective at winning prison inmates to Jesus Christ.

Inspired by Mark 16:15, his goal is to go into all parts of the world and preach the gospel to every creature, extending his ministry globally. A true evangelist and also a stage-four throat cancer survivor, Minister Johnson is an overcomer who has won many souls to Christ in street ministry, prisons, and serving those in need with old-fashioned witnessing.

After inmates are released, he maintains personal contact and has been remarkably successful at preventing their recidivism and helping these men to build productive new lives.

Minister Johnson is the youngest of four sons by the late Rev. Holloway Johnson and the late Maxine Louise Williams Johnson. He grew up in Tulsa, Oklahoma, and is the third generation of clergy in his family. However, before he realized the value of his family legacy he became involved with gangs and this lifestyle led him into drug addiction and prison, beginning during his military service in the Army.

In 2004 he surrendered his life to Jesus Christ after a dramatic encounter with the Lord and he joined a church that not only welcomed him but also gave him a vision for his God-given potential for an effective Christian ministry, The Father's House in Norcross, Georgia.

God began to speak to Minister Johnson about reaching out to those who were living in the places where he had been delivered from—prison and the streets. Thus, he began ministering in adult prison systems, juvenile detention centers, county jails, group homes, and places with at-risk kids.

He volunteered at alternative schools and mentored youth in the Gwinnett (Georgia) Public School system.

As a child of a mentally ill mother, he also developed a heart for those who have mental and emotional challenges.

He has never turned back to his former life and uses his experiences to reach people with the Gospel.

Minister Johnson resides in the Atlanta area with his dearly beloved wife Marya. He is the father of two sons, Alvin S. Johnson and Alonzo C. J. Johnson, who were murdered as victims of urban violence.

His sons' deaths as well as his own experiences in the streets have motivated him to bring a spiritual revolution that will change cities and restore people's lives.

"I highly recommend this life story by Minister Alvin Johnson as an inspiration of the miracle-working power of God. This is a man whose life has been fully transformed from a man in the clutches of evil to a righteous evangelist declaring the Word of God."

BISHOP GARLAND R. HUNT, SR.
Senior Pastor, The Father's House, Norcross, GA
Former President, Prison Fellowship

PRISON MINISTRIES

P.O. Box 920651
Norcross, Georgia 30010
www.Lethalweaponministries.org

ENDORSEMENTS OF ALVIN W. JOHNSON

THE IMPACT OF ALVIN JOHNSON'S MESSAGE IS CHANGING THE LIVES OF PRISON INMATES, former gang members, juvenile delinquents, and former addicts across the country and bringing them to Christ because of the credibility of his change. Through his Lethal Weapon Prison Ministries, he is personally discipling former inmates into productive Christian citizens.

Alvin has one of the most unique life experiences that I have ever heard. His transformation is much like that of Paul where he made havoc on behalf of the enemy and now he is making havoc on behalf of the Kingdom of God. I highly recommend this life story by Minister Alvin Johnson as an inspiration of the miracle-working power of God. This is a man whose life has been fully transformed from a man in the clutches of evil to a righteous evangelist declaring the Word of God.

The Bible says to honor those who labor among you. As his pastor, I honor Alvin Johnson as a man of God. He is the real thing in his life and ministry and I am pleased to fully endorse this book.

BISHOP GARLAND R. HUNT, SR.
Senior Pastor, The Father's House, Norcross, GA
Former President, Prison Fellowship

WHY IS IT THAT WISDOM COMES ONLY IN THE LATTER YEARS? I'm sure that if we polled a few people or one hundred, for that matter, we would get one hundred different answers. The reason I asked that question has to do with my baby brother, Minister Alvin W. Johnson.

When we were young, my brothers and I faced down the winds of wisdom in sheer rebellion. We were in opposition to everything but life itself. We were exactly what the Bible said we were, born in sin and shaped in iniquity. I myself was not a good example of what a big brother should be. I'm ashamed of myself that I led the way into smoking, drinking intoxicating beverages, and not just that but drug use, also. I was in a bike gang. Many times God spared my life.

A world-shocker for me was when I found out that my baby brother Alvin was doing the same things I was doing and in many cases was doing worse. Being street-smart and so-called slick, I never got caught or convicted for any of the many crimes I committed. With Alvin it wasn't so. Drugs convictions, handguns, shotguns, wine and women led him to prison.

In the meantime, God convicted me of my sins and brought me to himself in August of 1977. Then God placed me in the ministry. In 1997 I became the pastor of my childhood church, Northside Church of God in Christ here in Tulsa, Oklahoma. At that time, Alvin had gotten out of prison but was continuing his lifestyle of crime and deception.

In 2004, after I had loaned Alvin much money and received from him story after story (lies) about those funds and why they were needed, it came to me that I had "strengthened the hands of the wicked," as the Bible says. I decided to shut it down.

My brother called me on the very day that God revealed to me the misuse of the money that I had been sending him. His wife Marya called me sobbing and saying that Alvin had been lying to me. She explained that he had been buying and using drugs. She said to me, "I'm tired, David," her broken voice revealing over the phone the brokenness of her heart. I could feel her hurt as she spoke to me of how my brother's life was really messed up. I was angry!

When I finally talked to Alvin on the phone, I told him I wasn't sending him another dime. He said, "My furniture and all my belongings are out on the curb.! My rent hasn't been paid!" He pleaded with me long and hard, but I said "No!!" and hung up the phone.

He called right back! I answered the phone and again I said "No!" and hung up the phone.

The phone rang for the third time. I picked up the phone and was ready to slam down the receiver when I heard him sobbing. He was broken. This time I knew it wasn't a put-on. He wasn't faking. He had realized that everything was about to be ripped from his life.

It was at that moment that God registered in my spirit that a true change had taken place. So with a soothing in my heart and a calm in my mind, I loaned him what I had. From that time on, Alvin became a man of God.

Looking back with 20/20 hindsight, I can see that God was grooming Alvin for his prison ministry. The pain and sorrow we had with our mother and the sinful lifestyle we had led were meant for evil, but God allowed it for the greater good.

The Word of God is true. As Romans 8:28 says, "All things work together for good."

DR. DAVID J. JOHNSON SR.
*Pastor, Northside Church of God in Christ,
Tulsa, Oklahoma (Eldest Brother of Alvin Johnson)*

I AM SO GRATEFUL FOR THE LOVE AND SUPPORT THAT MINISTER ALVIN JOHNSON GAVE TO ME DURING MY EIGHT-YEAR INCARCERATION at Dooley State Prison and even more during his follow-up once l was discharged and living in the (ARC) Atlanta Recovery Center.

I remember how Minister Alvin used to bring the WORD in a real straight-forward way to the brothers and that got my attention. He never judged me or the charge I was forced to live with. He just kept it real with the word of GOD and that's what l needed to hear at that time.

The support he gave me once I got out was awesome. It showed me that he didn't just talk the talk but he walked it as well. My first dinner upon getting out l will never forget. Olive Garden, what a treat. But what really got me was his unselfishness to do this for me while he was fighting throat cancer. This motivated me to not give up on the vision God gave me to start Keeping It Real Ministry.

So, my brother, I wanted to let you know that those trips to pick me up from the center and taking me to your home for a guy's day out and going to service at your church were not in-vain. Today, four years later, because of God's grace and mercy and the people like you that are in my life, I work for KFC as a general manager of my own store, praise God. I'm in my own apartment with not only a car but also a brand new motorcycle.

Minister Alvin, the Bible speaks on giving honor to whom honor is due. With the same respect and warmth you showed to me I just wanted to give back to you and let you know that you have demonstrated First Corinthians 13:13. The Way Of Love.

GEORGE T GATES III
Keeping It Real Ministry (KIRM)
Stamford, Connecticut

I HAVE KNOWN MINISTER ALVIN JOHNSON FOR MORE THAN 10 YEARS, EVER SINCE WE BEGAN DOING PRISON MINISTRY TOGETHER IN 2005. I quickly discovered that there was something quite different about him from most other people I've ever met.

The more time I spent with him and learned about his life, I knew that God's arms were wrapped around him very tightly. I immediately realized that the passion he once had for the world he lived in with its debauchery that he had fervently sought out was now geared toward living for Christ.

Most people that I know would not have been able to overcome the trials that he has overcome. Alvin has made it his life's mission to win as many souls for Christ as he possibly can with that same ferocity he had while living as a sinner.

There's no question in my mind that Alvin Johnson has been given an assignment from God and he has embraced it with all of his heart, soul and mind. I've come to love this Man of God, and I'm honored to call him my best friend!

DAVID BRANDON
Associate Pastor, The Father's House, Norcross, GA
Former 11-year veteran, National Football League (NFL)
Co-Member The Father's House Prison Ministry Team

I FIRST MET ALVIN JOHNSON WHILE WAITING IN LINE AT A WENDY'S FAST FOOD RESTAURANT. IT WAS A DIVINE APPOINTMENT! God set up that meeting! I can still see his smiling face in my mind's eye.

As we waited in line, we talked about Jesus and I invited him to visit a church service at The Father's House. He took me up on that and the rest is history. Alvin started to grow in the Lord. He invited his wife Marya to start coming to church, and a great blessing was born!

Alvin felt a calling to start visiting the prisons. He returned to a place where he could be used of God to rescue many others with a background similar to his. For many years now he has been used greatly in leading many to Christ and to a new walk in discipleship.

I am grateful for his ministry, but what I love about this man is his love for Jesus! He has a tremendous desire to walk with the Lord and to share his love with everyone he meets. He is truly a man after God's own heart—a true, faithful, and authentic minister of the Gospel.

It's with great joy that I write this endorsement. I pray that the Lord continues to bless your ministry, your family, your life. May the book be a blessing to many!

Pastor Lawrence "Doc" Reed
Fellowship of International Churches

I'VE BEEN FRIENDS WITH ALVIN AND MARYA JOHNSON SINCE 1999 when I met them at the Extended Stay Hotel where I was working. Alvin has always been a funny and cool guy but he once had some demon spirits like a drug habit of alcohol and crack that took over his life and almost lost him his wife.

He used to stay out for days or weeks at a time during his binges and have everyone worried about him. Alvin had been put out of hotels one after another, but God had his hands on him. He was losing jobs one after another and spending all the rent money. Sometimes when we would drink together or hang out together I would see him smoking crack and I'd ask him why he did that. He would never respond.

In 2004, Alvin and his wife moved into an apartment and sometime during the month Marya called my wife. She was crying and saying they had to move because Alvin was at it again and took the money. We went to help her pack. During the packing and loading, there was no Alvin. Marya was crying and my wife was comforting her.

Then, while we were still packing, Alvin showed up and he was crying. He called me outside and said that he had seen a burning bush and that God was talking to him about his life.

Since then, Alvin has made a big turnaround and never looked back. Through it all, his wife never left him. Whenever he visits me now he is always talking about the goodness of the Lord. He ministers to me and my wife and friends. He's on fire now for the Lord.

Our friendship has grown to be like brothers. I love him and his wife. They're my family. You know, there's a saying that people come in and out of your life for a reason. We are rooted in there with them to stay.

John 3:16 says, "For God so loved the world he gave his only begotten Son." God bless you, my brother!

CLIFTON PRICE
Long-Time Friend

JUST A SMALL NOTE ON MY RELATIONSHIP WITH MY CHRISTIAN BROTHER, MINISTER ALVIN JOHNSON. I believe he is a true man of God! When I first met him, I thought, *"This guy talks too much!"* However, after getting to know him I found out that he always says things about people that would bring glory to the name of Jesus, except when he thinks that everyone in the church should help to keep it clean, and even then he says it would better exemplify a Christian's behavior.

Knowing a man like Alvin makes you want to keep yourself humble before the Lord. He has given his whole life for the Gospel. He is a soul-winner. He believes that all should live a life of purity for the Lord.

I really enjoy listening to him now. All he talks about is doing what God wants for himself and you! You have to love him for the sake of Christ. His favorite Bible saying is "And why do you call me, Lord, Lord, and do not the things which I say?"

When I hear him preach in the prisons, I know that he understands that the people are blinded. Their lives mean a lot to us and we let them know that no matter why they are there, Jesus still loves them. Their way to freedom is through living a life given over to the Lord Jesus Christ!

CLAIRE CARTER
A Sister and Mother in the Lord
Elder, The Father's House
Co-Member The Father's House Prison Ministry Team

1720 East Woodrow Street
The Alvin W. Johnson Story

ISBN-13: 978-0-9847821-9-2

Printed in the United States of America
APPTE Publishing, Atlanta, Georgia
"We Publish the Fivefold"

P.O. Box 920651
Norcross, Georgia 30010
www.Lethalweaponministries.org

83177613R00072

Made in the USA
Lexington, KY
09 March 2018